THE PROMISE OF THE FIFTH SUN

ANCESTRAL JOURNEY OF SELF DISCOVERY

DR. JORGE PARTIDA

The Promise of the Fifth Sun
ANCESTRAL JOURNEY OF SELF DISCOVERY

For my grandmother and *madrina* Lidia, a powerful *curandera*.

To Amanda Dominguez

David Dominguez

Eric Dominguez

To Crystal Partida

Daniel Partida

Jonathan Partida

To Dalilah Partida

To Eliazar Partida

And to Jacquelynn Partida

To Nicolas Partida

To Francisco Partida Jr.

To little Ava and to Nina Partida

To all the Children of the Sun, present and future.
You are the light of the world.
You are proof beyond a shadow of a doubt, that the Promise of the Fifth Sun
has been fulfilled.

I wish to express my deepest and most sincere gratitude to Harini Riana for her faith, support and willingness to come along on this journey.

PREFACE

The past few years, leading to the writing of this book, have been most challenging and personally transformative. I have been led along a search for myself that has taken me to dark and desolate places I long ago thought I had conquered. I have experienced a gradual, and sometimes painfully sudden, falling away of an old identity to which I had previously clung to like a drowning man does to a raft. My old self, infused with ego and a billion insecurities, was an identity that organized my place in the world and dictated my relationships. Frustrated with everyone else and wondering what was wrong with the world, I came to the painful realization that the real problem laid with me and no one else. The realization has left me cold and often scared. Many past acquaintances are no longer in my life, and loneliness has often gripped my very heart and soul. Yet, there is also an excitement I have not known before, as I realize for the first time, just how much of a stranger I have been to myself and how much greatness there is yet to be discovered. My life thus far has been epitomized by one constant attempt to be liked, to be successful, and to be the best. I have tried to be the All American good boy, working hard to please others. I have been the big brother and surrogate father to my brothers and best friends, but I have not known to just be content with being myself.

In moments of despair and confusion, the voices of my ancestors have come to guide my journey. It is in following my steps back in time that I have come to have a deeper and more significant appreciation for my past. It is in the avoidance of the same pitfalls of the past, that I have been able to move forward with grace and courage. I recognize the past infused in every grain of dirt of these California lands and in every frozen drop of water in the harsh Chicago winters. I feel the influence of the ancient spirits stir in my bones. I step on hallowed ground that still breathes in the souls of those native ancestors whose blood I feel stir in my own body. The whisperings of my ancestors tell a different story of the universe and its creator. This story is abundant, peaceful and joyous and it outlines a different way of being in the world than the way I have lived in past years.

Tracing Back

I was born in Mexico and grew up in Chicago where I studied and obtained my doctorate in clinical psychology. I always knew that healing, helping and following the spiritual path, were ideals that called to me from a time and place before my birth. While children learned to say "mama" and "papa" as their first words, mine was *misa* (mass). As a child, I found great comfort in the old churches and while other children played cars, I played I was a priest saying holy mass.

Yet, even beyond the sorrowful and painful faces of bleeding and weeping saints, I could also see the traces of fierce ancestral gods, hiding their face and identities behind the bright clothing of Catholic saints. Something about the mystery of the unseen, something about the purity of spirit called to me and drew me to study TRUTH in all its manifestations.

Later, frustrated by the shortcomings of traditional psychology's inability to explain and include a perspective that spoke to my experiences, I studied under various *curanderos* (healers) in the Mexican states of Chiapas, Michoacán and Guanajuato. These healers have confirmed what I have always believed. The power to heal cannot be separated from the stories we adopt as our own. The truth of illness or cure lies in the belief system of each individual. In order to appreciate a different perspective, we must suspend our own assumptions. The greatest and most challenging lessons have arrived when the light of truth has chased away the shadows formed by the lies I have lived. The closer I am drawn to the great mysteries of life, the more my own life has seemed to come undone, until the point where I am left raw and exposed. Life seems brand new and I am still catching up, learning how to be in this new world with the new legs and wings I have sprouted.

As a psychologist I have labored my entire professional career to bring together and bridge the wisdom and teachings of my ancestors with the Western theories that I have studied and have taught. I strongly believe in the intuitive knowledge that is carried in our bodies. I believe in the wisdom of the ancestors that speaks to an eternal and ever present intelligence of love and healing, of wellness and wholeness. The ancestors' way represents a healing and liberating wisdom that is as old as time itself. Holding on to my truth and learning to speak my word has often meant I had to stand alone. In so doing, I have often incurred the wrath and disapproval of my profession, my colleagues and friends. Yet my aspirations are not for power or for fame. I am convinced that what is humbly written in these pages is nothing more than the universal truth that is our collective human inheritance.

The Journey

I look at my own story and can't help but wonder about the force and miracle that has brought me this far. Surrounded by poverty, addiction, crime and despair, I have allowed myself to be guided by an internal voice and a force that I recognize as the voices of my own ancestors and, most particularly, the old teachings of my grandmother.

I grew up with two childhoods. From birth to the age of eight, my family lived in Guadalajara, Mexico. When I was nine years old my family moved to the suburbs of Chicago and to a very different world. Along with the bitter Midwest winters, I also experienced the cold reality of what it meant to be a Mexican living on U.S. soil. My parents and grandparents had taught me that being Mexican was a source of pride. However, as I learned what *spick, wetback, greaser* and *beaner* meant from children my age who shouted and threw their kicks and punches at me, I quickly realized that the teaching did not quite translate in this land that is supposed to be of dreams and endless possibilities. Whenever I felt lost and confused, I could always hear the voice of my grandmother whispering in my ear, "Child, be still. Stay true to yourself and your family. There are many false stories that are told which can change the very base of the human soul."

Every individual of Mexican descent, no matter how far back their Mexican heritage is traced, cannot help but be vulnerable to the influences of history and distorted myths. History and the experiences of past generations have deposited their collective memory in our minds. We integrate these lessons so automatically that we seldom question if these lessons still apply to life today. When we adopt a notion of ourselves, of life and the world, based on distorted perceptions of our own worth, we are likely to feel inferior without ever fully identifying the cause or source of this inferiority.

This book traces the steps that you and I and all our ancestors have walked along the journey towards self discovery. The book is structured to reproduce the physical, mental and spiritual journey of life which every human being must fulfill. Along the path, the experiences of those that came before us are available as myths and legends. These experiences fall into the category of "race consciousness". This is the information that is passed on to us from one generation to the next. We may not be aware of these lessons, but they are there, hidden in the very make up of every one of our cells. As you travel along this journey of self discovery, you will learn to reclaim everything that you have ever lost along the way. When you have a clear picture of the path already behind, you will be better able to see the destination before you. You will then have the power to direct the course of your own life. It is never too late to reclaim the joyous, abundant life that is rightfully yours.

Hope

I believe that there is a healing our world desperately yearns for. It is the healing required in order to bring about a different understanding of our relationship to each other and to the delicate world we inhabit. I speak of ancestral pride, not to participate in a division of peoples, between us and them, but quite the contrary. I hope that such pride will allow us to recognize the unity of our experience and the oneness of our family.

This book is intended for all who stand for truth and choose to walk in the path of reason. It is dedicated to anyone, regardless of national origin, regardless of color of skin or religious beliefs of creation. My sincere hope is that the message contained in these pages is useful to you as you embark upon the reclaiming and rediscovering of your intended journey. Go forth in search of your truth and meaning, and the abundant life that eternally stirs within your own soul.

Dr. Jorge Partida

PROLOGUE

The Myth of the Fifth Sun

This is the mythical story left to us by the *Nican Tlaca*, the name given to all people who are native to this continent now called the Americas. The Olmecs, Toltecs, Aztecs, Mixtecs, Zapotecs, and many other *Nican Tlaca* nations, share the same creation myth. The ONE CREATOR, who is equal parts male and female, carved the world and molded life out of chaos and darkness. It came to pass, long, long ago, before the birth of time that Father-Mother Creator (known as *Ometecuhtli-Omecihuatl*) gave birth to the four gods, the four directions, the four divine powers known to us as Water, Earth, Fire and Wind. As a gift, the Creator gave to each of his four children the opportunity to rule over life, to be the sun governing over the world they created. The four gods were young and immature, quick tempered and impulsive. In their need to prove their superiority and dominance over the others, the world was destroyed. Four worlds existed and four worlds came to destruction. Competition, hunger for power, jealousy and over blown egos caused the destruction of all life on four separate occasions. Without balance and harmony, without cooperation and coexistence, the four gods experienced the loss of their most cherished possession. The four gods witnessed the destruction of their own creation.

Finally, ashamed and defeated, the four gods met in *Teotihuacan* (the City of the Gods) to request from the Creator one last opportunity to bring life into existence. The Creator scolded and reprimanded the children; but being ever kind and generous, the Creator granted the wish of the children for one last chance at managing life on a new earth. Such creation would, however, require a sacrifice. The Creator asked for the gods to step forward, directing that one of them would have to sacrifice himself to become the Fifth Sun. The Creator built a great fire and asked his sons to walk into it. The handsome God of Wind (Quetzalquatl) stepped close to the fire but then stepped back in fear. It was the God of Fire and Will Power, the noble and humble, uncelebrated god (Huichilopotztli) who jumped into the fire without hesitation. Faith in the words of the Creator transformed the gesture of sacrifice into Tonatiuh, the mighty God of the Fifth Sun who rules over this, the fifth and final world. Through faith and belief, the great become so much greater.

Tonatiuh is the Father of our modern times. He is the God of the Fifth Sun, the god of spiritual transformation and self realization. His is the face we see staring back at us when we look at the round stone of the Aztec Calendar. If we look at his tongue sticking out, we will see that it is in the form of a blade, signifying his sacrifice and the sacrifice of countless others that has been required for us to arrive at this point in our lives.

In the four directions of the stone is the representation of each one of the four original worlds. The worlds are represented by four separate inter-circles going from the center outward to the edges of the stone. The four circles are full of symbols and seem to rotate and revolve. These are the four previous worlds which came and went, destroyed because of imbalance, frailty and attachment. Yet at the core of the stone is Tonatiuh, constant and consistent, solidly staring back. His face looks boldly forward, showing that the fifth world does not change and is not governed by time, appearance or movement.

The Promise of the Fifth Sun

The kingdom of Tonatiuh is the promised kingdom of *Nican Tlaca*, members of the original family, who trace their roots back to the beginning of all life. We are all their descendents, the children of the Fifth Sun, intricately connected by history and culture. More than 25,000 years ago, our ancestors came from Africa to Asia and across the Bering Strait into the Americas by way of the north. Many years after, our great grandparents left the mythical lands of Aztlan to follow a dream of prosperity and abundance. Across cultures and ages, our ancestors wandered and were guided by myths of a promised land. They finally came upon such a promised paradise, where, as it was written, heaven and earth came to meet. Upon that place, they built the grand city of Tenochtitlan, the present day Mexico City.

Our Aztec ancestors built the grand city right on the spot where the eagle was found devouring the serpent. In the story, the eagle represents the heavens and the serpent represents earth with all of its darkness and confusion. Heaven and earth met on that very spot and the entire experience of human creation was transformed instantaneously upon witnessing the foretold myth become reality. The light of the heavens conquered the darkness and ignorance of our fears and we were transformed. We were transformed yet again when two separate worlds, the European and the Native collided, forever altering humanity.

The serpent, representing our fears and doubts is devoured by the eagle, which represents the deep power of the heavens and the universe as well as our soul or our inner potential. The serpent is that part of the self which is weighed down by doubt, uncertainty and limitations, but the eagle is the promise of spirit, of unrealized potential, of the creative, healing, restorative force which is found at the center of our being. Mexico City not only represents the birth of the modern movement with technology and the changing world market economy, but it is also a place of great spiritual significance where the ancient gods and Christianity speak with equal clarity, promising the transformation and liberation of those most oppressed. In the Mexican experience, in the lives of all that are descendents of that nation, ancient and divergent worlds, cultures and mythologies mix and mingle to express the complexity of our human existence.

In the old days, the *Nican Tlaca* predicted that in the final fifth world the secrets of life and liberation would be revealed. This world would be marked by great change, destruction and transition, ruled by *Ollin*, the god of change and turmoil. *Ollin*, usually pictured as an animal skull with large fangs, feeds on the proud accomplishments of our fragile human condition, particularly as we strive to hoard material possessions and power. It is written that the Fifth Sun will rule over this present time of great transformation. Although there will be great confusion and suffering, particularly for those who resist the natural and impersonal universal principles, there is also the simultaneous potential for the greatest evolution of human consciousness, self awareness and enlightenment.

This is your life. It is the life of this fifth world, governed by the light of the Fifth Sun. This is your world and my world. It is the world that was foretold in great detail, etched in stone and carved across the face of the great Aztec Calendar. These carvings, which illustrate the promise of the Fifth Sun, guarantee true freedom in your lifetime. True freedom can be found inside your own mind. You simply have to remain true to yourself. Maintain guard of your mind and your thoughts and do not allow negative experiences of your past to invade your present life. The instructions included in this book are intended to bring your life into harmonious balance so that the external changing forces do not come to govern your inner peace and do not dictate the quality of your life. Once you know your true origin, you know the power you hold to impact this universe. There will be nothing you cannot accomplish!

TABLE OF CONTENTS

1

Myths: Past, Present and Future

What is a myth? A myth is an ancient traditional story, or a series of stories, usually about heroes and supernatural beings. These stories often attempt to explain the origins of natural phenomena or aspects of human behavior.

Myths are often told as attempts to explain the origins of human behavior, a culture's world view which includes spirituality, natural phenomena, cosmology, aspects of healing and the very meaning of life and human existence. Myths are not just entertaining fables or children's stories told to pass the time. Myths represent a blueprint to the psychology of a people, their understanding of themselves as a group and their view of the world and the universe. Myths therefore, reveal a personal perspective regarding the evolution of history and culture. Our history is mixed with our culture, tangled in our spirituality and is lived in and as our present experience of life.

Who you are is made up of the stories you heard about your family, your background, your culture, your religion, your gender, and the reasons for your very existence. This interchange and exchange of concepts and traditions produces a psychology that is truly unique in its simplicity and its universality. This psychology offers a native perspective of wellness which emphasizes, not the importance of the self or individual experience, but rather, collective contributions which now seek expression and recognition in and through your embodiment. In other words, myths offer an explanation for who you are in connection to the universe you inhabit. They explain the reasons why "you" have been created and they also teach about all the previous "others" that it took to make "you".

Myths are so deeply engrained in the human psyche that when tampered with, or right out deleted, they can alter human behavior and the view of life. By integrating a false story that changes the meaning of who you are and what you are worth, you can come to believe that you are unworthy. This is a total distortion from mythical origin tales which express the collective truth of your birth as a direct descendent of the Creator.

Another definition of myths includes the representation of something that is fictitious or non-existent, but whose existence is widely believed by a group to be the truth. As an example, historically Jesus was not born on December 25th as is the commonly celebrated myth. Look up birth of Jesus in any encyclopedia or in any scholarly book on theology or even an internet search and you will read that Jesus was born sometime in September or October. We all celebrate his birth in December, but that is a myth. This celebration in December became popular as a result of the increasing dominance of Christianity over the old Roman religion. Romans celebrated the birth of the Sun gods on December 25th. To most people, it doesn't really matter when Jesus was born as much as it matters that he existed and had a message. Pagan cultures, which were overcome by Judeo-Christian tradition, celebrated the winter equinox and the start of a new year. A December birth combines Judeo-Christian tradition with ancient pagan rituals and creates a new standard practice. The conquered people find themselves celebrating new traditions superimposed on ancient, buried traditions which today have lost or distorted the original meaning.

Another example of an altered myth includes the concept and image of God which was superimposed on native people when the *Conquistadores* (Spanish conquerors) arrived in the New World. The new arrivals felt better about their actions when they were able to convince themselves that the natives they encountered were somehow less human. Because natives were considered savages, the *Conquistadores* felt they could "save their souls" by destroying the ancient concepts of the Creator. The native gods, rituals and celebrations were considered "idolatry," an offense against the ONE true religion and thus punishable by death. It is much easier to kill, enslave, colonize and oppress others if you don't have to think of them as human. The problem of identification with oppression does not disappear with time. Today, many descendents of natives from the Americas, from Asia and Africa, still internalize these myths of oppression and consider themselves inferior, largely based on the mythical concepts they have adopted from a dominant culture. How many times have you looked at someone (including yourself) and judged according to color of skin, texture of hair or any concept of beauty based on a Western ideal? Where do you think these thoughts of inferiority come from?

History is written by the power holders and the dominant. That version of history produces one superior myth, one version of reality which is sold to everyone as the ultimate truth. In that process and in that story, the popular view of history typically dehumanizes and minimizes the contributions and moral character of those conquered along the way.

It is no wonder that the children of the Fifth Sun might think there is little value in knowing the myths and stories of their ancestors. Myths of ancestors can be thought to be "superstitious" or "primitive". We might believe that the natives were nothing but savages who had little appreciation for human life, civilization, culture and progress. As the stories of our past disappear, so do the important lessons, the teachings which stress the need for living a harmonious life and living by the principles the ancestors taught to thrive and survive. If we learn to read the stories of the past and recognize their significance in our present lives, we will be able to decipher the messages that are imbedded in the myths and creation stories which have been told for thousands of years.

Myths: The Lessons

Myths teach us a great deal about people and their beliefs. They tell us how people view themselves and the world they inhabit. Myths give us an understanding of a group's aspiration towards fulfillment. The teachings imbedded in these myths show the values and ideals that are crucial in the preservation of a way of life. Myths can provide us with stories to relate to and relevant messages to guide our lives. We all know about Oedipus, the king who married his mother and killed his father. This myth has permeated history and psychology, giving us a theory of understanding (however controversial) about the manner in which boys in Western cultures relate to their mothers and fathers.

At times, I have felt like *Sisyphus*, a Greek mythological character, who was condemned to roll the same rock up and down the same hill for eternity. Other times I have felt like another Greek mythological character, *Icarus*, a son of a god, who flew too close to the sun only to come down to earth in a burning blaze. These myths teach me about my thirst for union

4

with the Creator and the catastrophe that can occur when flying too close to the sun. I learn from myths that I have not been the only one in creation to ever feel this way. I learn that the moral teachings of yesteryear are valuable lessons today. As an example, from the story of *Sisyphus*, we can learn to step back and observe patterns of behavior that can trap us forever in a "hell" like environment. From the story of *Icarus*, we learn that pride and arrogance can quickly become our downfall. The fact that you are more likely to know these myths than the myths of your ancestors indicates how your morality and personal stories were formed. If you adopt a script not intended with you in mind, you can believe in an identity that distorts your true worth and significance.

Our lives and our culture have been shaped by these myths. From the legends of King Arthur to the stories of the Gods of Olympus, myths have become a part of the collective story we tell of ourselves and others. Myths inform our aspirations, fears and cultural norms. They give us insight into our hang-ups and fears. Yet, for those of us that are descendents of the ancient native tribes, the traditional myths from Europe do not fully reflect our reality. When people are unable to see themselves reflected in the majority culture, there is a sense of being discounted, invisible and unworthy. Others might see you as different and you learn to base your sense of personal worth on the majority's view. Seeing yourself through the legends and teachings of your own ancestors gives you a more valid and accurate view of your place in the universe. The lessons in the stories of our elders can empower us with unimaginable wealth, wisdom, joy and health.

Our Stories

Myths contain the lessons of the past which still have their present teaching and significance. These lessons are a collective

5

inheritance of past successes and failures found throughout human existence. Our own individual existence is not separate from the history of our people or the history of the entire world. There is an intuitive and physical body of knowledge that has been inherent to us by the collective and the individual lives of all those that have walked this journey before. All your past relatives have contributed and given of their lives to form the person you are today. For generations upon generations, the hopes and aspirations of our ancestors have resulted in the embodiment of our individual lives. We are the life and love, the hope and aspirations that the elders projected into the future. There are unimaginable riches left behind for us, accumulated by the nobility and passed on by the royalty of our ancestors.

The importance of living a balanced and harmonious life is a teaching which survives in the stories and in the healing rituals of the old *curanderos* (healers). Our ancestors, while they were building great pyramids and studying the movement of the planets with mathematical perfection, were also engrossed in the study of human life - our lives on earth and beyond. They charted the unexplored regions of the mind and the body, and left you and me the wealth of their accumulated knowledge. They took clues for living and for survival from their observations of earth's and the universe's rhythms. They praised the earth in recognition of the forces of nature that governed their lives. Their life's work informs us of our place within the cosmos. This knowledge was intended to be passed on to the children of the Fifth Sun so that we could utilize these universal principles to our greater benefit and to secure our happiness and ultimate fulfillment.

Our ancestors were powerful healers who understood there is no separation between wellness of the body and wellness of the mind. They understood that our health and well-being depends on the balance of our physical, psychological and spiritual nature. The path of life for our ancestors was simple, although not necessarily easy to follow. Our elders recognized the importance of living close to the earth and they were protected by a canopy of celestial bodies. They knew that a personal and social balance with all universal and natural forces was critical for fulfillment. Living in harmony with animal and plant spirits held the key to wellness and was intricately related to the preservation of that balance and harmony. The dance of harmony assures the continuation of all life.

Our elders believed that we are trapped by the illusion of change and separation. In a world where everything changes and nothing stays constant, the human race began to hunger for permanence, including a permanence of the self. Such permanence is an illusion whenever it is anchored to the material world. The more we attempt to hold on to a sense of permanence, the more frustrated and disappointed we become. Try trapping a river with a bucket. You might be able to hold a bucket of river-water as a constant, but what you have is only water and not the river.

Today, remnants of these ancient myths are found in popular culture. Messages and guideposts from our ancestors are also imbedded in the melodies of old songs that speak of morality, our resilience, and the heroes that have given their lives to secure our survival. Great examples of these songs are Mexican *rancheras*, a genre of the traditional music and *corridos*, a popular narrative story sung in poetic rhyme. *Rancheras* are more than song and poetry. They represent the oral history and tradition that the children of the Fifth Sun continue to utilize to preserve a way of life. *Rancheras* are the Univision and Telemundo of the past. They are the poor person's version of the daily journal that tells about the news and scandals that occurred nationally and regionally. Not only was information disseminated through these songs, they also expressed values, ideals, dreams and aspirations of past generations. The *Mariachis* express the angst and the striving experienced as Native and European cultures mix and seek expression in our lives. At times, we live as Jose Alfredo's "El Rey". We may not have a throne or a queen but we are still the king! Other times, the same Jose Alfredo declares that "life is worth nothing." It begins with tears and ends with tears. The highs and lows that describe Mexican and Mexican-American existence have never been better captured by any other cultural icon than Don Jose Alfredo.

We learn about past laws and the harsh, punitive stands taken. From the song "La Martina", we learn that infidelity was punishable by death, particularly if you were a female who just "completed her sixteenth birthday". The song "El Hijo Desobediente" teaches that disobeying your parents can condemn you for eternity. These songs attempted to teach natives the ways and laws of the Western conquerors. The songs tell the stories and experiences of individuals as they attempt to integrate new, strange and oppressive practices into their existence. Soon, the children of the Fifth Sun began to forget their connection to the ancestral past. Continuing to read and write within the native tradition became acts punishable by death. That is why those ancient traditions and teachings are all but physically extinct. Yet their message, their intention, their purpose and meaning are not lost. These are spiritual principles that operate beyond the limitations of the material world.

There are clues that point the way to the liberation of your own oppression. These clues are hidden, but they can still be found when you learn to tap into the ancestral and intuitive field of knowledge. Such knowing is charted in the path of the stars pointing to the ancestors' discovery of the stairways to heaven. To unlock the ancient secrets we need only remember that the clues are hidden within the center of our own knowing. In silent meditation, you can still hear these messages whispering in your ear. These clues help us understand how to avoid the holes in the ground that can drag us to our own personal hell. More importantly, these clues tell us how to climb to the highest point of self realization and then think and act from that perspective.

The ancient myths are also hidden in stories told repeatedly by your grandparents and mine. As they surround themselves with numerous children, the rich and vivid details in their story telling illustrate and celebrate the tales of our origins, back when the world was still young. The messages imbedded in these myths and legends reveal the secrets necessary to find the true story of "who we are". In the appreciation of the legacy of our ancestry, we will find the lessons necessary to avoid pain and suffering. As we rediscover the transformative messages, we will personally feel the ancestral pull that unites us to the source of all power and creation. These are the stories that tell of our place in this universe and the purpose of our life. The messages will unlock the code to our happiness and allow us to claim our rightful inheritance.

Your life sets the decisive tone and theme of an ancient story written exclusively in anticipation of your arrival. The past has been lived as a gift to you, so that you can select and interpret reality based on the lessons you've inherited. If you are disconnected from the myths of your past, you are likely to feel as an illegitimate child, unaware and unclear of how to act and behave. You are more vulnerable to material influences which tend to discount the rich ancestral heritage. This heritage contains great wisdom and the secrets to fulfillment of your most cherished desires. This heritage represents an unbroken chain of love and affection that reaches from the beginning of time right down to your individual manifestation.

You are the legacy of the past and the creator of the future. You were intended to be free, to live in joy and prosperity. Five hundred years of oppression and colonization have left certain scars, but these scars have not touched the essence of who you are. At the core, you are as complete today as you were the day you were born. You have everything you need to live beyond fear and limitations. The journey to the promised lands of Aztlan, to the realm of unlimited possibilities, can be realized by breaking the chains of self imposed suffering and oppression. Come along, let us take this journey together and discover the significance of the promise of light and liberation entrusted to you.

2

The Beginning

The great mind that ever thought of every idea and the great heart that ever felt every grand emotion are undivided parts of the ONE. All the love and joy, all of the health and wellness, all of the riches we can imagine, spring forth generously and instantaneously from the ONE. Every idea is contained within this ONE. This ONE has always been so great and grand that no words have ever successfully described it. The ONE has always been more awesome than any person can imagine. From itself and of itself, the ONE created the many expressions. From the beginning of time to the present, right down to our very own lives, the ONE has lovingly watched as its creation becomes increasingly more aware of itself.

The very purpose of our lives on this planet is to embark upon a journey of self discovery. This journey propels us forward so that we might uncover our actualized full potential. Your potential is already imbedded at your core and to uncover it, you must start with an understanding of the beginning of the thing you call your *self*. We must have some sense of our beginnings to keep sight of our destination and the original intention set for our existence. Great things await you because your ancestors lived, worked and died to assure that great things flowed to you and from you.

The experience of being human, the experience of consciousness, has always been a collective striving to understand the source from which we all emanate. Since the beginning of time our ancestors have lived in communication and celebration with existence. To our ancestors, life was an endless dance and a constant celebration in honor of the unseen power. The gods of the ancestors are merely different disguises and embodiments of the Creator. The eternal spirit of life takes on human feelings and reactions because human experience is the ultimate frame of reference available to best explain and define the unseen. The unseen power of creation expresses itself in human form and human consciousness attempts to explain that which is beyond human understanding. Our ancestors observed that nothing can be called "good" without having some reference to its opposite. This story of opposites plays strongly throughout Aztec mythology. The legend of the identical god-brothers, Quetzalquatl and Huichiloptozli, is such an example. The identical gods share a deep and powerful bond. They can be at peace or they can experience turmoil that takes them to extreme reactions. As they are mirrors of each other, they must guard such a delicate balance. They are subject to competition, rivalry, jealousy and envy. These competitive and powerful forces often keep the two brothers divided and out of sync with the natural harmony of the universe. The love they have for each other is fierce and intense, but it is just as intense as the mistrust each holds towards the other. If they move too far from center, they cannot remain apart for long. Their reunion is a sweet melody and their subsequent separation is always intensely tragic.

Quetzalquatl is the god of mirrors, the shape-shifter and trickster. He is the dark shadow side of his twin, Huchiloptozli, who is the god of will power. The brothers are mirror images of each other. Love and hate, pain and pleasure, the longing for and the fear of love we often express simultaneously. It is said that long, long ago, the brothers were separated from each other for hundreds of years. The children of the gods wept and suffered the separation and the lands lost their abundance. The lands and the descendent children waited patiently for the prophecy to be realized with the reunion. Quetzalquatl promised his return when the world is ready to receive him. It was Quetzalquatl whom the Aztecs thought had returned to claim his rightful throne when the *conquistadores* arrived in Mexico. That was the reason why the natives offered no resistance. Were the Aztecs, the children of Huichiloptozli, correct in believing Quetzalquatl had arrived? Did Quetzalquatl, the shape-shifter and trickster, come to reclaim the Aztec throne? Are the Aztecs and the *conquistadores* twin brothers meant to be united in a thunderous clash of opposing forces?

The notion of right and wrong, dominion and oppression, good and bad are concepts determined by our individual experience of life. The *conquistadores* believed they had a God-given right to claim everything they found in the name of the king and the church. They believed that they were saving the souls of the savages. The Aztecs believed that their power and dynasty would come to an abrupt and inevitable decline until their descendents, the children of the Fifth Sun, awoke to a higher awareness and self realization. Given their respective myths, both cultures are correct and both perceptions of reality are equally valid. Which version of reality do you claim as your own? What is your personal myth of transformation?

There are many ancient myths that teach us how paradise is lost and how paradise can be reclaimed. In these myths there is always a time of perfect harmony, which is violated by some human shortcoming. In the biblical beginning of human existence, disobedience of God's rules caused Adam and Eve to be expelled from paradise. Students of this myth learn that disobedience means eternal damnation. There is another myth which the ancestors told of the time when paradise was lost and the children of the Creator were made to wander in the desert. Both tales illustrate the mystery of human evolution. There is a "chosen" separation from the Creator only to return with a heightened sense of connection and gratitude.

The elders say that more than two thousand years ago, a group of traveling young men was invited to stay at the peaceful and elegant kingdom of an old and wise Toltec ruler. The ruler's heart was full of love and compassion. Feeling for the wandering youth, the ruler offered his daughter's hand to the leader of these young wanderers. The arrogant young leader accepted the princess' hand. The noble king was filled with joy and showered the young travelers with gifts and treasures of all sorts. The young leader thought the old ruler to be a fool. On the couple's wedding night, the young man skinned his bride alive and danced around all morning wearing the skin of his bride to be. The old ruler, grief-stricken, shocked and broken hearted, expelled the youth and his followers from this paradise. The group wandered for many days and months. In the loneliness of the desert, the wandering tribe had to cleanse themselves of the horrible tragedy. The young leader of the group had a vision of forgiveness and redemption. Now repentant and older, he dreamed that the group would wander for many years, lost and miserable until they would see heaven and earth connecting and uniting as one. This would be a sign that goodness would once again rule over the land, conquering ignorance, lack and limitation. The symbol from the dream was manifested as an eagle, representing the heavens, eating a snake, representing earthly attachment, ignorance, greed and limitation. The group of youth was the *Mechicas*, the Aztecs who came to build their great empire in Tenochtitlan, right on the spot where they saw the eagle devouring the serpent. That spot is now Mexico City. What do you think our ancestors meant to teach us about hospitality, gratitude, humility and the importance of peaceful co-existence?

Although our Aztec ancestors thrived, building great cities more grand than any European city at the time, in the collective race consciousness, there was always the memory of the atrocities that marked the birth of the nation. Similarly, in our Bible story of Adam and Eve, humans are left to wander the earth, marked by original sin that resulted from the expulsion caused by disobeying and insulting God. The Aztecs lived with a constant collective fear that the Creator would be pleased with a sacrifice of what humans most valued, which was their own life and blood. Just as Jesus willingly gave of his blood for all to exist, the Aztecs willingly gave of their own blood to secure the continuity of life. According to ancient mythology, life occurs in cycles and everything repeats itself in similar themes. Life has a way of always balancing itself. Some cultures call this the law of Karma.

The Aztecs were deeply connected to their source. They also had a prophesy which declared that one day they would open their door in hospitality and know the experience of a guest who turns against a generous and trusting host. More than five hundred years ago, these children of Huichiloptozli, the Fifth Sun, looked toward the ocean waiting for the fulfillment of what had been foretold. When the *conquistadores* arrived, the Aztecs believed it was Quetzalquatl returning to reclaim his throne. Just as in the myth of the youth who betrayed the generous king, the Aztec ruler found himself turning his kingdom over to his guests and in that manner, another cycle of life was completed and the prophecy was fulfilled. Huichiloptozli and Quetzalquatl, the brothers, were reunited, but the old rivalries and injuries were re-enacted. The worlds of the *conquistadores* from Europe and the tribes of the Aztecs collided violently. In less than one decade of the arrival of the

15

conquistadores, most of the native Aztec population was dead. The memories and experiences of our ancestors, who lived through that violent clash, are carried in our collective memory. Even if we are not aware, we are still living out the modern consequences and the impact produced by that collision of cultures.

By embracing the *conquistadores* as gods, the Aztecs were fulfilling the prophecy. The myth of the twin brothers reuniting thus came to pass. Yet, there is one more myth to be fulfilled. This is the myth that speaks of the inevitable awakening and the quantum evolutionary leap that the children of the Fifth Sun are about to realize.

In this story of the two gods, Huichiloptozli and Quetzalquatl, Huichiloptozli represents our truer, higher self, while Quetzalquatl represents the investments we make on our false sense of "self." All of us get caught up in the glitz and glamour of an ego that just cannot be satisfied, no matter how many toys and how many things we collect in life. Remember that the two gods are mirror images of each other and each is the shadow side of the other. From this myth we see how the ancient concept of *Enlaketch* is enacted in our daily life. *Enlaketch* is the Toltecs' and Aztecs' belief that each one of us is a mirror reflection of the other. "You are my other self." When you say you hate someone, you project your own sense of inadequacy on the person you hate. In other words, you dislike in someone else what you dislike about yourself. People can only show you a reflection of your own perceptions. People are mirrors, showing you only what you project, whether such projections are parts of yourself you like or dislike. The other notion of *Enlaketch* is that we are all connected, whether such connections are readily apparent or not. The oppressor is connected to those who are oppressed. Likewise, the oppressed can only be liberated when he or she chooses to no longer participate in the oppressive relationship. Our ancestors believed that every person and every experience in our lives are constructed knowingly or unknowingly by our own mind and by the mind of the Creator in order to teach a lesson of deeper love.

What do we do to invite aggression and abuse in our lives? We must recognize that revenge and rivalry never result in peace. We can continue to be angry and wish revenge upon those that we perceive to have caused us harm. Holding on to our anger and resentment only makes our life smaller and limits our ability to be truly happy. We must recognize the face of our other self in those we meet. The hatred and resentment we feel towards another most often is merely self resentment toward the issues we have not resolved. As the children of the Fifth Sun, we must recognize that we are a mixture of two worlds coming together. You are equally half *Nican* and equally half European. You are simultaneously your oppressor and the oppressed.

While it is true that we've lived a long history of oppression and that such long history leaves its indelible mark upon our development, we don't have to allow our past to be our future. So many times, we use the past as an excuse for our present limitation. We tell ourselves we cannot achieve, we cannot move ahead, we cannot be happy because of what happened to us yesterday. It is within our own consciousness and identity that peace and understanding must be obtained. We cannot continue to live with internalized hatred one minute and an oppressive sense of self importance the next. Therefore, we must work to unify dueling aspects of our own identity in order to obtain peace.

When Humans Are Not Able to Relate to Their Image of the Divine

When the *conquistadores* arrived at a "New World", they killed the elders, burned the books and eliminated written expression. Without written information, knowledge was passed from the elders to the young by word of mouth. Although this was neither the most accurate nor the most efficient way of learning, the elders took great care to memorize in fine detail every word of every major text they were able to save. Soon the old native languages were outlawed. Violators who insisted on speaking their native tongue were killed and people had to learn a new and strange language or suffer death. The languages, the songs, the melodies and teachings of native voices grew faint until they almost disappeared. The old temples to the primary gods were destroyed and atop the ruins of the old, the faithful children of the native land were forced to construct grand cathedrals to the new religion and the new saints.

Out of the need to maintain control and oppression, conquerors imposed their perspectives and views of the Divine. Not surprisingly, the image of the Divine tends to always favor and look a great deal like the new rulers. These new rulers feared and vilified the religion of the natives and made every attempt to destroy all evidence that any other mythology of the Creator ever existed. Along with the native images of the Creator and the Divine, the new rulers also made every attempt to eradicate the cosmology and the mythology of the entire conquered culture. The new religion taught that the native children were to serve and suffer in this life. Humility, sacrifice, and self denial were considered external demonstrations of faith.

As the children of the Fifth Sun, we cannot help but believe the myths of the dominant culture which repeatedly teach that the ways of our elders are at worst wicked and at best superstitious mumbo jumbo. The concept of the Creator and the Divine represents the collective experiences of a culture. Suddenly, the Creator seemed to have one type of relationship with those in power and another, very different, relationship with the oppressed. When the conquered elders looked upon the face of the new Creator, they no longer saw a reflection of themselves. Instead of seeing their concept of the Divine, they saw the faces of the new arrivals who dominated by force and threat. The Creator became something to be feared; and in that fear, people were controlled with threats of hell and eternal damnation if they did not obey the keepers of power.

Our native ancestors were forced to hide their images of the Creator and the old healing ways within the clothing and wooden bodies of the new Catholic saints. Rituals and healing practices of the old world became incorporated into the new prayers and religious teachings. Somehow, the ancient teachings, the old healing ways endured and the old faith and practices continued. The transformative healing of old *curanderos* endured and their knowledge and practice was carried onward, entrusted carefully from one ancient healer to the next generation. One healer hand-chose a worthy pupil among the awakened few; and upon this open mind, the old healers planted the seeds of their art and belief system. That is how *curanderos* still exist. These healers represent a mixture of the ancient traditions, now mixed with the teachings of the new European religion.

Like the conquering rulers of the "new world", the imported concept of God was of a being who was directly inaccessible, punitive, harsh, critical, resentful and judgmental. The colonized were to kneel down in obedience, humility, sacrifice and unworthiness. This mythology taught us to lower ourselves before God and before those who seemed to have ready access to his ear. It soon became a crime to follow the old traditions. To insist was a demonstration of resistance and therefore punishable by death. God became the means of oppression and the evidence of dominance.

There has always been ONE power of creation. If there is only *one God*, then isn't the God of our native ancestors the same God of our European ancestors? Every culture celebrates the Creator in the best way the group can conceive of such power. The natives knew that the mighty power of the Creator manifested itself in and through all of creation. They saw the face of God wherever they looked, in the trees and plants, in the animals, in the stars and in themselves. To take away their ability to adore and praise their concept of the Creator meant the certain death of their entire race and ancestry. That is why our native ancestors risked it all for the survival of the faith and the path.

There is no greater damage that can be inflicted upon people than to control their minds. By controlling the native culture's mythology, rituals and faith, the dominant culture had an ability to control the destiny, the minds and bodies of those who were now servants and workers. When any entity other than yourself holds the power of your original thought and creativity, you cease original thought and your sense of worth is negatively impacted. Your frame of reference shifts to fall in line with the status quo. Soon, you can easily feel you are an object or a victim with no hope to transcend your perceived limitations. You no longer hear the faint voice of your intuition and inherent power because you start to believe that the mythical "reality" superimposed on your external world is more real than the power your mind has to transform the world. You can begin to believe you are powerless to change your external circumstances. Of course, that simply is not true.

Our ability to feel powerful, to feel that our individual life matters, is a result of our ability to see ourselves in direct relationship to a force greater than our own personal life.

Whether you are an atheist or religiously inclined, the belief in a greater power existing in and all around you, coupled with the realization that you are in direct relationship to that force, gives you access to the source of that energy and power. This belief also gives you the ability to impact the world in a significant manner as a direct agent creation.

When our native ancestors were forbidden to adore their previous understanding and conceptualization of the Creator, their understanding of reality and of the universe was altered. The Creator of old was a reflection of the people and had native features, traits and attributes. The Creator of old understood well the needs and aspirations of its children, but the new Creator required compliance and assimilation into an entirely separate reality and conceptualization of the world. What happens when the distance between our lives and the creative force is brokered by other individuals and institutions? What happens when we internalize a concept of God that is punitive and harsh?

This new conceptualization of God changed the relationship that the native ancestors had with the Creator. Such a concept of God maintained the new world order as it formalized the distance between the dominant new arrivals and the remaining native inhabitants. A societal hierarchy based on race and color was established and the native ancestors became objectified, seen as little more than a cheap workforce with limited rights. If your native ancestors could be seen as less than human, then there could be little discord or remorse in treating them as such.

These bad habits, unfortunately, tend not to stay buried in history. Instead, these bad habits make their way into much of today's social structure and they are passed from one generation to the next without much critical analysis. We tend to hold many beliefs that are hateful and critical of ourselves and of others without recognizing that we've inherited many of these beliefs without scrutiny. We tend to see ourselves as objectified when we allow others to treat us less than we deserve. We participate in our own objectification when we engage in behaviors or thoughts that we know are damaging to us. We objectify others when we mistreat them or use them for our own pleasure and purpose. By robbing ourselves and others of our inherent humanity, it becomes easier to hate, to abuse and to mistreat.

This mistreatment is performed without conscious awareness since the collective memory of our ancestors' past is so deeply engrained in our collective mind. We are seldom aware of just how powerful these thoughts are in our mind. These deeply buried beliefs and experiences affect our relationship to ourselves and they also dictate the quality of our lives. We must, therefore, unpack the inherited mythology of dominance and oppression. We must know our own story and begin to recognize the myths of inferiority which have shaped generations of our past and present misconceptions of life. The myths of oppression must be discarded so that we may re-establish our direct connection to the liberating power of the Fifth Sun.

Our Curse: The Myth of Separation and the Myth of Limitation

As the ancient myths of ancestral people were replaced by the new myths of the colonizers, the natives began to incorporate the themes of inferiority. The natives were taught that anything that was good was outside of them. The right to happiness, love, abundance, peace, justice and all worthwhile human pursuits were the birthright only of the dominant class. The role of the natives was now to assure the happiness and success of the people who had invaded them. Throughout time, these messages still reverberate as they are transferred from one generation to the next. Today, you may not be aware to what level you have incorporated some of these false teachings, but they are buried in your mind, creating barriers to your happiness. These myths can be challenged and your mind can be redirected to adopt a more positive script that is in line with your true inherent potential.

Many believe that self awareness is humanity's greatest gift and is also our greatest curse. Humans are the only animals on earth who are ever conscious of their mortality. Myths across the world are filled with stories of humans attempting to overcome their mortal limitations. In native traditions, when the Creator was upset, then rain did not fall and the earth did not produce. In Judeo-Christian mythology, God was upset and took the gift of paradise from humans, expelling them to suffer illness and death. From Egyptians mummifying their royal dead bodies to Jesus' promise of an afterlife for those who believe, cultures across the world have struggled to understand and transcend the limitations of physical death. The Aztecs tried to transcend this limitation by throwing themselves at the sacrificial stone in an attempt to prove that death was an illusion. Many of us still live life afraid to truly live, not realizing that it is not death we fear, but life.

Omar is a thirty-four year old man from Michoacan. For years he has been suffering from extreme nightmares and an intense fear of dying that won't let him be at peace. Omar spends much of his time going to doctors to make sure he is not developing cancer or other serious illnesses. He has also been going to a dermatologist and has had several surgeries to remove a burn scar from behind his calf. He is convinced he is unattractive and that somehow everyone who meets him focuses on the scar they can't really even see. After some time, Omar revealed that, as a child, he received serious and repeated beatings from his alcoholic father, who would wake him up in the middle of the night after coming home drunk only to abuse him with a belt.

Omar's intense fear of dying stems from his past suffering and unwillingness to discuss and address issues stemming from the suffering he endured during his childhood. He hungers for the life and the unharmed ancestral potential that stirs within him, strong and radiant. Omar is frightened of that power because he cannot understand it and because that power feels so different from the pain of life he has come to know as reality.

Because the ancestral force within Omar is strong and feels so opposite of what he has experienced as life so far, Omar fears that what stirs within him can only be death. The ancestors won't stop caring for Omar. They know the weight of responsibility placed on him; but more importantly, the ancestors must now deliver on the promise they made to Omar, their "mas pequeño de todos mis hijos", (smallest of all my children). From the perspective of the ancestral journey, Omar must forgive his alcoholic father but only by healing himself first. Once Omar is able to tap into the force behind that ancestral power, he will be able to move beyond fear, pain and suffering without having to die first to obtain it.

How different would our lives be if we believed that life is eternal? The native ancestors believed that death was a thin barrier. That barrier could be crossed willingly at any moment of choice. By such penetration, death is exposed as a trickster and liar and therefore we can all live life more completely, unafraid of the lies of death.

Death is the greatest proof of our belief in fear and limitation. Death would mean a termination of consciousness. Yet, consciousness is not bound by time or space. You can project your thoughts to the past, to the future or to the present. The concept of superposition in quantum physics teaches us that one object can be present in multiple places at the same time. The same field of study teaches us that the observer is not separate from the object that is observed. The observer, rather, determines reality by what the observer chooses to observe. Until you fix your attention on a certain object or idea, everything else before and after exists merely as a field of potential possibilities. In other words, you create your reality! The possibilities for your life are endless, limited only by your perceptions and by what you choose to limit yourself. Consciousness is the material, the essence of creation and as such, it is not limited by space, time, or even physical death.

Across the span of time, humans have rebelled against death, the ultimate perceived flaw in the divine plan. To feel secure we have developed a ferocious appetite for material possessions in a futile attempt to obtain permanence. Power and dominance thus became the standard measure by which cultures proved their superiority over earthly existence. In order for some to have a great deal more, others have to have a great deal less. The more people have, the more they tend to want. The more things people collect, the more it becomes necessary to create protective borders around accumulated wealth so that others will not steal or retaliate. Hoarding material wealth and power makes people fearful, suspicious and mistrustful. You hoard because you believe that power is external to you. You grab at everything, fearing you will be left without. This is giving into the myth of lack and limitation. The universe has proven that it is governed by a law of abundance. The stars and planets are infinite in number and there are billions of grains of sand that cover the smallest beach. With this in mind, how can you focus on what you don't have? If you focus on what you don't have, you will have trouble believing that good is truly unlimited. In reality, what you are able to perceive is limited by your own perception.

For generations we have all bought into the myth of separation, lack and limitation. Yet, the ancient concept of *enlaketch* and our own modern understanding of consciousness both teach that the perception of another is merely a reflection of our own thoughts and self perception. You cannot perceive anything that does not stem from your own understanding. The myths of separation and limitation create a false perception and view of the other as an enemy. You defend because you are a product of an extensive history of conflict and struggle. Your ancestors had to fight constant oppression in order to survive. Collective and historical guilt and mistrust create a present fear of retaliation or injury.

Invading cultures across history learned to hoard by convincing themselves of their superiority over others. They attempted to create a false sense of security but lived in constant fear of retaliation from those they had oppressed. Our native ancestors believed that everyone comes into the field of our perception because we somehow called them into our life. All of us are connected and so all of us share in every experience of oppression or liberation. Perhaps the most obvious evidence of our inter connection is witnessing the collective harm to our environment. If we continue to mistreat the environment, we all face the same fate.

What is possible in your life? Whatever you dare imagine! Whatever you dare believe! The world is limited only by your perception. Expand the capacity of your mind to think beyond what you believe is possible. Hold your desires as a constant in your mind without concern for how such desire will come true. Our native ancestors believed that conflict and fear were a gift. They are mere illusions designed to test the strength of our convictions. You would not appreciate what you have accomplished if everything was easy and conflict free. If you truly desire something, then you keep watch over your thoughts and reject any appearances to the contrary. You will be a witness to your desires manifesting in time.

The history of creation, of the world, of your ancestry, has gone through a great deal of trouble to assure your survival. All of these efforts have been necessary and worthwhile because they have brought you into existence. Your existence is essential. The universe waits for you to contribute and write the next chapter in the continuing saga of our human evolution.

Our Evolving Understanding of the Divine

As our human consciousness evolves, so does our concept and understanding of the creative force which is in back of all things. Judeo-Christian tradition begins with a wrathful and temperamental God who asks for sacrifices of first born children, who punishes and expels his children from paradise, and who kills and punishes all those who do not fall in line. Aztec mythology viewed the Creator as requiring sacrifice of life, that possession which humans held as most precious. To the elders, there was no separation between humans and gods. At any moment, anyone could realize an eternal union with the Creator by willingly ripping away the thin veil separating life from death. Across the span of time we've come to understand that our collective concept of the Creator evolves in direct relation and proportion to our own abilities to understand love, compassion and kindness. You project your own limitations onto your concept of a Creator, but the Creator is ever loving, giving, and forgiving. The field of creation always says "yes" to whatever thoughts you project onto it.

The lessons of history have their present significance. These lessons are a collective inheritance of past successes and failures found throughout the experiment of human existence. Your own existence is not separate from the history of your people or the history of the entire world. The stories and myths of every culture have valuable lessons for your daily living. Keep in mind however, that truth is often in the eye of the beholder and in the words of the writers of history. Whether you consider the myth of Adam and Eve, or the myth of the Aztecs searching for the promised lands, both stories tell of a time when creation and creator co-existed in peace and harmony, but the desire for self expression expelled humans to search the world for their own definition and formation. We seldom reflect on the indelible mark which history and evolution leave upon our collective and individual life. Without such reflection, we are condemned to repeat the same mistakes time and time again. Today, we understand that our own consciousness and our own thoughts are closely linked to the creative force that governs our universe.

Lesson: This is a Good Day to Clean Up

Ancestral myths and family legends dictate the point of reference for experience and orientation. Your dreams, aspirations and longings are rooted in legends you heard from a far-away past or the recent past of your immediate family of origin. You are susceptible to the many inconsistent messages to which you are exposed. Some of the early stories you heard about your family and your background may not be very positive; and so, you might learn to question yourself and to doubt your potential. If you can't believe what you hear or what you see, you can come to question and doubt everything. Your mind learns that something is not right, but it doesn't know exactly what is wrong. To assure it misses nothing, our mind takes in everything it perceives so as to resolve some unknown crisis that it senses but can't identify. Your confused mind now feels separated from the good that surrounds you and you feel separate from the giving universal force.

Believing the myth of separation, humans have wandered the world in mistrust and fear of punishment. The once united human family has dispersed and siblings have turned against each other. Lured and seduced by hoarding of goods, riches, and external appearances of power, brother has turned against brother. In this process, it is easy to forget our origins and the intention set behind our existence on earth. When this happens, it is hard to see where we are headed. Without knowing where we are going, how do we get what we need to reach our destination? We must always be aware of where we come from and keep a clear sense of where we desire to go.

Knowing that no obstacle can obstruct our inherited divine destiny, we can more easily determine what we need to have in order to unleash our true potential. Knowing that we are capable of greatness, we can select and discern with purpose and intention. So often, in a society that is obsessed with hyper-achievement and intense self focus, we accumulate and grab just out of fear of not having. Every choice that comes into our field of perception appears to be a possibility. In a universe of endless possibilities, discernment allows us to let go of those possibilities that only lead us into dead-ends. Grabbing at everything that comes our way soon becomes a heavy burden. Our minds are soon bogged down by so many unnecessary things that we have accumulated along our journey. It is time to clean up! Along the way you've picked up thoughts and practices that weigh you down. Make a commitment to lighten your load. Later on, you will learn a systemic process to identify harmful thoughts and begin a process of letting go. On this journey, it helps to travel light and with a clear sense of direction.

3

The Power of the Mind

By understanding the creation myths which come from our culture of origin, we can begin to unlock the secret code to our true identity. We can forge strong connections to our past and thus know that our present awareness represents an ancient promise which is just now being fulfilled. The ancestral past becomes a source of strength and leads to a greater sense of personal awareness and a greater, deeper notion of "you" in relation to the universal creative force, or the Divine. The lessons handed by the wisest healers of our ancestral past understood that the window to eternity and the secrets needed to break the barrier between the material and spiritual world laid in the evolution of our human consciousness as this awareness is the most powerful evidence of a "Creator". Understanding the creation myths of our culture gives us a direct connection to the observations and to the relationship our ancestors had with the universal power of creation and transformation.

History tends to be a biased account of events as recorded and remembered by those in power and authority. We, who are descendents of a history of human oppression and slavery, are impacted by a heritage of false and obliterated teachings. Along the many years of distorted teachings and the manipulation of history, you have come to adopt false beliefs which do not reveal your true worth. By consciously or subconsciously adopting these myths, your actions begin to reflect those false perspectives. Your life then becomes limited by the negative and false teachings you have integrated as truth of your identity. You can change those internalized stories if you know where and how you have integrated these false teachings. Your mind has adopted a script based on a distorted understanding of your origins. By adopting such a script, your mind limits your ability to transcend your current situation. Your adopted script limits the capacity of your mind to evolve beyond that false script. By knowing your ancestral past, you can learn from and adopt the original teachings. These teachings place you in the center of the universe and declare you as a direct descendant of healers, rulers, sages and fierce warriors. You have the power to change your mind and change the script that you've adopted. The ancestral hope for your life is imbedded in the collective race consciousness which is found within the very fabric of your mind. If we understand the teachings of the past, we can observe our own life within this context. We can understand and decode, through the tales and messages of our ancestors, the guidance needed to live a full and balanced life.

Your life, your identity, is organized as a series of concepts and ideas familiar to your mind. You learn by repeated exposure and experience. Life is lived according to the power of your mind to hold one consistent view of the physical and emotional world which you inhabit. When you encounter something new, your mind must determine what similar past experience it has on file. The new experience becomes labeled as "good" or "bad" based on your past experiences. Yet, your mind might hold past experiences which were passed on by ancestors who suffered great pain and mistreatment. You can adopt those same feelings of oppression and never know where your pain comes from, unless you unlock the false teachings of the past.

THE POWER OF THE MIND

Go back far enough and you will learn the story of creation prior to oppression, when your ancestors existed on the same plane as the Creator. In ancient Toltec tradition, it is said that the elders in Teotihuacan were direct descendents of the Creator and lived in peace, abundance, wisdom and eternity. The voice and the presence of the Creator were observed in every person, plant, animal and element. There was no separation between God and the reality of everyday people. People knew how to read the signs and blessings in everything and in everyone they encountered. We have lost that ability to commune with creation because we have adopted a different way of seeing the world. In essence, we have adopted a different "filing system".

There are many factors that contribute to our filing system. Your view of life is your individual filing system that is made up of assumptions and assessments you have integrated about your worth and that of others. Those of us born under a history of oppression and colonization, tend to have incorporated strong, persistent messages of inferiority and unworthiness. Some of us have incorporated these messages to a greater degree than others, but we've all been infected. The issue is not to blame or to fear, but to clearly assess the place where you've been stuck and determine that you will have the courage to move forward.

Oh, it is not easy! You might even have to let go of many memories you have used to define your identity. You will fight and struggle, but if you persist, you will see your life changing, evolving before your very eyes. In fear, often you will tend to resist. No matter how good your life can be, you won't allow yourself to believe it! Why? Simply put, because you have been taught and worst yet, you believe that you do not deserve goodness!

Many generations of our elders were taught they could not wish for more than to suffer as a cheap labor force. Many of us still carry the burden of these false teachings. With awareness, what you previously believed to be the truth now becomes a simple miscalculation of the truth. Armed with a new insight, you can identify and question problematic beliefs and behaviors which stem from false teachings. Once you identify, you can embark on changing those "bad" patterns. At first, new behaviors will seem uncomfortable and strange. There will be a push for you to go back, to "regress" to past behaviors. Hold firm. If you work on solving the erroneous thinking pattern, even to the point of addressing the emotions, fears and desires that arise, you will find that your perception of the past and the present begins to lighten up. Soon, new behaviors begin to form a healthier routine.

You can learn to face your past with courage and gratitude. No matter how troubling this past has been, you can decide to move forward with grace into a greater today. Your individual past, your childhood, and all of the pain and fear that you still retain can all be transformative factors that will allow peace and joy to enter your present life. Unlock the meaning of your past and take hold of the key. As rewards for your efforts, you will come to experience a fuller relationship with every element that surrounds you. You will understand the reasons for your attachment to pain and suffering. You will know how your past inability to forgive was caused by an understandable lack of trust. A deeper understanding will set you free and will stimulate your inevitable growth and transformation.

The Inferiority Complex

Being the direct descendent of more than five hundred years of colonization and oppression has a direct impact on the manner in which you identify and develop a sense of self, family and community. The discovery of the "new world" was fueled by the hunger for accumulation of riches, power and wealth. This approach created fear, defensiveness and a fragmented world in which everything is quantified, categorized and manipulated in an effort to control and dominate the perceived enemy. Those in power have always believed the myth that the Creator has given them special privileges to govern over everything and everyone. Religions have claimed their superiority over other religions by arguing that they are God's "chosen people". Kings in history claimed their legitimacy by creating the myth that they had been "divinely appointed" to rule over all. People gave in to oppressive rule because they believed themselves lead by someone specifically appointed by God. They forgot that the true Creator is personal and resides in the center of the evolving human consciousness. During a time in history when the Cross and the Crown were in an all out war for control of lands, riches and people's minds, their hunger for dominance lead to the "discovery" of a new world. The competition for power intensified between church and state. The church threatened people with excommunication and death while the state took lands and wealth from those least capable of defending themselves. The ground for the greatest battle between church and state consisted of dominance and suppression of the "savages" and the import of slave labor.

A dominant society assigns its expectations to every individual within its confines. Each individual's worth is determined by their proximity and relationship to wealth and power. We are all treated based on the expectations our authorities have upon us. Our teachers, our bosses, and even our parents, treat us based on their idea of a "preferred outcome". That preferred outcome is based on the majority's view of power, beauty, race and merit. Those that more closely represent the majority's ideals are considered more desirable and powerful. However, such concepts are also based on myths adopted by the majority who are in authority. As a child of the Fifth Sun, you are likely to be reminded constantly of your status as a "minority". The label implies that you are of less importance, of less merit, but the label is based on myths that are not of your ancestry.

When you are cut off from the myths of your culture of origin, you are likely to experience great psychological suffering and confusion because society's personal myths are not in line with the actual circumstances and realities of your own life. You may not be aware of your suffering, but you begin to give in to a lesser version of your life's potential. You feel that the "minority myth" does not fit your life, yet you cannot pinpoint why that is. Like many other people, you may come to believe the majority myth and act from that false notion of self. You might feel that you are less deserving, less intelligent, less attractive, less capable, and less human somehow. Often, when I visit junior high and high schools, many Latino children say that they feel left out and picked on. They say they often can't relate to what they are learning and feel stupid, afraid and bored. It is easy to see why so many students drop out, withdraw or retaliate, believing that they are less intelligent than others. You may never even be aware of how or when you incorporated false notions of your true worth. You are likely to feel incomplete, as though only half of your life makes sense. By missing the significance of the myths and rituals left by your ancestors, you may be missing a bridge to your deeper self.

Without the teachings of your elders, you will tend to make unnecessary mistakes and you will hold on to limited understandings of your true capacity. You can walk along this earth without a clear sense of direction, like operating an expensive piece of equipment with no instruction manual. Let this book be your owner's manual. Within the subsequent pages you will find material previously deleted but necessary for the development of a liberated self awareness. The material now inserted is intended to complement your understanding of health and wellness. This understanding of wellness is not compartmentalized. In our dominant culture, we've come to divide health and wellness into separate categories which include mind, body and spirit as distinct compartments. Our ancestors understood that wellness is integrated and includes an approach which reclaims the person as a whole being-possessing mind, body and spirit as integrated and indivisible entities.

Myths guide us along our path in life, creating models and bridges between our conscious and unconscious life, between the past and the present. Myths are more than legends. They represent the philosophical and religious models used by cultural groups to organize perceptions, thoughts, feelings and actions. The famous psychologist, Carl Jung, spoke about collective archetypes, the symbols and myths that influence our identities and which are passed on to us as a result of history and past generations.

Consider our concept of modern psychology. Many of our current notions regarding human behavior are based on our understanding of mythology -- European mythology. Freud, for example, describes the drives of human desire by making reference to certain Greek and Roman myths. The erotic, passionate love impulse he described comes from the Greek myth of Eros, or the Roman Cupid, striking lovers with his arrow. Freud also stated that there is a Narcissistic self-obsessed development in humans, borrowing from the myth of the boy who falls in love with his own reflection in the water. There are countless of other examples where our current understanding of modern psychology can be directly traced to ancient myths. Yet, these theories might explain how behaviors and personalities develop within a Western European heritage, but they do not offer universal prototypes for how distinct cultures have developed across the world.

Do these ancient myths create a screen upon which we project our experiences? Do they describe our understanding and expectation of human nature? Television is our modern myth maker. When I was a child and new to life in the United States, I used to watch "The Brady Bunch", believing that they represented every "American" family. Imagine how inferior I felt when I saw my family being and behaving so differently than the friendly and perpetually happy family on television. There are also six siblings in my family, but our story is very different indeed. What if there has always been more than one way to understand the evolution of life and of human consciousness? What if the descendents of indigenous peoples and the descendents of European Anglo-Americans truly live in two separate realities? What if different myths dictate a different path of life?

Internalizing the Oppressor

You tend to be more familiar with the European part of your background and heritage because that has become your dominant culture. Today, a dominant European perspective is not limited by borders or continents. In Mexico and everywhere else in the world where tribal heritages are an element of identity, young people often adopt physical features and trends which are more in line with a foreign, but more "popular" culture. You may even feel a certain shame about the blood of the tribes that runs through your veins and may downplay its influence instead of celebrating its presence. This tendency to block and minimize what and who you are causes you to see only half the world through half a lens. Because you see only half of all there is, you tend to bump into objects and walls, inadvertently keeping and blocking yourself from your own power and good.

For hundreds of years those of us that are a mixture of both cultures or who identify more with the proud native heritage of our ancestors, have been given persistent messages that we are less capable, of less worth than our pure European brothers and sisters. Many children learn from adults to hate others who have darker complexion, or because others have different hair texture, or because others don't believe in the same things. Many children also feel excluded because they don't "belong". Many "minority" children fail to conform to a school system that uses "standardized testing" known by all authorities to be culturally invalid. However, our students are still judged as being learning disabled or failures simply because they learn differently and are shaped by cultures and perspectives outside of the "standard" realm created by the dominant culture.

The fact that we learn these oppressive and distorted messages about our worth is damaging indeed, but much worse is the fact that many of us have come to secretly believe the obvious false teachings contained in these messages. A history of colonization turned the land, previously regarded as a mother, into property. Those that were born on these lands were stripped of their home and their way of life. Generations later, we still find that "minorities" tend to have less access to housing, employment, education and other opportunities. We are still living out the historical consequences of oppression and dominance. Is this because we believe we are less deserving? Are our lives still controlled and dictated by an internal or external "oppressor"?

We are still treating each other just like the conquerors treated our native ancestors. Do you hate your brother for being darker than you, or for being a new immigrant to these lands? Hatred is just as powerful when it is externalized as when it is turned inward. When you look in the mirror, what do you see? What do you say to yourself? What do you feel you deserve? Do you hate your size, the color of your skin, or the texture of your hair? If you do, you are likely holding on to damaging messages from the past. These false beliefs about your identity become internalized in your mind and body and they are acted out in daily life.

You make decisions to interact and react, depending on the messages your senses receive. Your decision to react or not react to your environment is based on many factors, including how well you feel you can be accepted by the majority culture, how you feel about your own culture of origin, about your family, and your own abilities to navigate this society. If you believe you will be accepted as an equal member, you are likely to desire blending in. If you believe that no matter what you do, you will be rejected by the majority of society, you tend to rebel and adopt a defiant attitude. Regardless of your choice to react, act or not act, you create the world you inhabit. If you choose to defy authority, this defiance will get you labeled a trouble maker sooner or later. Once you are labeled, there is a growing myth that is created about your identity. You become a source of irritation and it seems you cannot walk into a room without feeling watchful eyes following you, just in case you decide to act in an unpredictable or violent fashion.

It is time we recognize that we inhabit two worlds with two different views about life and our connection to it. In the majority perspective, we must divide everything we perceive into measurable and quantifiable parts that can then be controlled and marketed. In a native world view, we tend to hold a perspective that focuses on the interaction and relationship between all elements. This view is integrative and tends not to divide or compartmentalize. How can you divide the complexity of the perceived world? How do you hold life still long enough to break it apart and sell it like used car parts?

As children of the Fifth Sun, we have learned from our ancestors that the universe is a tapestry of perspectives. Each fabric is a new color or detail added on to magnify the beauty of the quilt. The mistake that you can make is to determine and gauge your sense of self worth in response to the acceptance or rejection of others' approval. If you work hard to change popular opinion of yourself, you will assimilate to others' desires for you; but once you comply, you are no longer your own person. You are now an individual whose concept of self is largely dependent on someone liking you or approving of who you are. Why would you want to place yourself in a situation where anyone else holds power over your potential? At this point, you have internalized your own oppressor. You don't need anyone else in the world to put you down. You are quite capable of doing that yourself, thank you!

Internalized oppression occurs when we become just like the power that we feel is controlling and directing our lives. When you feel abused or mistreated, you begin to act like the persons or institutions you feel inflict harm on you. When you feel oppressed, you feel wounded and reactive. In anger and pain you might decide to withdraw and not react. You may decide to harm yourself somehow. You may even choose to find someone you perceive to have less power than you, or someone who is in a more pitiful situation than you. Feeling righteous and justified in your anger, you tend to inflict the harm that has been inflicted on you. Your blind spots cause you to inflict harm on yourself and on others. Such blind spots keep you from realizing the extent of your actions. When you don't feel good about yourself, you tend to be your worst critic. If others treat you with resentment and hostility, you tend to view them as right and yourself as wrong. You tend to be punitive and mean towards those individuals closest to you. You retaliate against the face you see in the mirror. Your negative action towards others separates you from the rest of the world. When you judge "them" for excluding you, you have proven your own misguided theory of separation and inequality.

Taking personal responsibility for your actions, reactions, and for your own thoughts, is one of the most challenging tasks you will ever have to overcome. To take responsibility is to recognize that you've participated in creating your own false myth. To recognize error in judgment represents a blow to your "ego". Your ego instantly perceives any criticism and potential shortcoming as a blow to its integrity. Like a child, your ego feels the need to defend itself from perceived threats. In that fashion, your ego reacts by finding an external situation or person to attack. You focus on an external explanation for your perceived shortcomings and you lash out against that externally identified threat.

In other words, when you feel an internal shortcoming or inadequacy, you look for someone or something to blame first. When you feel criticized, you tend to personalize the criticism and feel the need to defend yourself. In defending yourself, you either withdraw or lash out against others. If you withdraw, you become depressed. If you lash out, you become angry, bitter and anxious. It is much easier to see the perceived problem in someone else than in yourself. You project your anger and resentment towards the one who most reminds you of your shortcomings. You attack in the other that quality or trait that you find most repulsive in yourself. As our Toltec and Aztec forefathers taught us, the other is *enlaketch*, our mirror self, a reflection of our own projections. Lashing out and attacking only highlights the issues that you still need to resolve. These issues represent the darkest fears you must battle the most.

Perhaps the harshest discovery you will have to confront along this journey of life is the realization that your greatest enemy looks just like you. Recall the myth of Huichiloptozli looking into the face of his mirror, his brother Quetzalquatl. Sometimes when you look at yourself in the mirror, it appears that your distorted self looks back at you and criticizes your shortcomings. You are confronted with yourself and the image of yourself. You judge that one of these is good and the other is bad. You split that reflection of yourself and tend to see all that is undesirable as not part of you. You split from all that you perceive as bad and say, "That is not me." It is much easier to see whatever you do not like to see inside you as being outside of you. Look in the mirror and say, "I am deserving of all the goodness in life," and in time these statements will change your life. Good thoughts have the power to manifest a better world just as much as bad thoughts have the power to create a harsher and crueler reality. If you hate, your hate is a reflection of you, of your fears and your uncertainties. Your hatred is not a measure of the person that is the focal point of your hatred, but a measure of the growth you still must undertake.

In an effort to distance yourself from your perceived enemy, you exaggerate the differences that separate you from "them". Yet, these differences are always superficial and subjective. Learn to let go of hate and release those you have held responsible for your hatred. Write a better story of your past and become actively involved in the creation of your improved reality. Take the driver's seat. Above all, learn to be gentle with yourself and reward yourself when you identify patterns of thought that previously harmed you. Release, let go and embrace your new heightened sense of awareness.

Competition

Why do you compete? What do you compete for? You compete for anything because you have been taught that goodness is available in limited quantity. You identify the enemy that is keeping you from your good. You then begin to strategize a plan to battle your enemy. The battle rages on and on. Exhausted, you come to the realization that competition might get you where you want to go, but the real question becomes how much have you had to pay to get there? Often, you become overly competitive because you feel as though you must fight others for the crumbs of shrinking resources. We treat each other as if the other were taking what life intended for us. One of my fondest memories of childhood in Mexico is sitting at the table with everyone present for dinner. We would grab our tortillas from the central basket. Each child grabbed the piece they needed and threw the rest of the tortilla back in the basket for the next person to grab. Today, we all act and believe that there is only one "tortilla" to be shared amongst our people and we must fight each other to get that tortilla for ourselves. Where is our extended family connection? Today, how are we helping our "compadre" [1]? Have we lost each other to the myth of lack and limitation?

We create borders and barriers designed to keep others from threatening our hoarded fortune. Ultimately, we are all still fighting for crumbs because we fail to recognize that the positive and good in the world has the potential to exist with equal abundance for everyone. If you become convinced that in

---

[1] A compadre, literally means a co-parent. This is the title given to the chosen family relative. The honored person becomes a godfather to the child of a beloved friend. In so doing, the honored person becomes a part of the intimate family. The bond between compadres is unconditional, eternal and universal.

this world of plenty there are limited goods and resources, you come to view your mirror self as the enemy. Your mirror self is that person that most reminds you of yourself. That is why often as Latinos, we can be most competitive and punitive among ourselves. As I visit largely Latino high-schools across the nation, I am saddened to observe that our young men and women are often being taught to kill themselves in the name of the "cause". In my work with gangs, the "cause" has come to mean this troubled notion of liberation and retaliation by any means necessary, including death. Our young men and women say they are fighting for La Raza, for culture and tradition, but they are also pulling the trigger that ends the lives of the one most like themselves. Using bits and pieces of history, from Cesar Chavez to the Aztec traditions, our young are often unaware of the significance of our legacy and are easily manipulated for power and profit. Our young people are repeating an old ritual and spiritual passage by giving their lives for the perceived survival of self and others. Yet, we must erase the hold of that myth because sacrifice is no longer necessary.

Do you celebrate when your neighbor runs into good fortune, or do you see yourself as being upset the good fortune did not happen to you? Watching your brother get his good fortune takes nothing away from you getting yours. Quite the opposite! The closer abundance comes into your personal circle the more likely you are to become its next grateful recipient. If you are joyous for someone else, your mind is letting you know that it is capable of recreating the desired experience. Your mind then goes about setting matter in motion so as to create a real live stage on which you can project your joy. A focused mind recognizes that the feeling of celebration is familiar and pleasurable and so it seeks to recreate the experience again and again.

If you are envious and jealous of someone else, you are really judging yourself as incapable of manifesting that goodness for your own self. You are likely to want to take another's happiness or abundance away because you doubt that good could come right to you. That action of jealousy and envy directly diminishes your opportunity for progress and abundance. You begin to feel the world is unjust and unfair and your thoughts begin to create the world you envision. Limitation is a myth that we must unlearn. The truth is that we live in a universe that is abundant and generous. There is no limit to what we can have; no limit to what we are capable of accomplishing if we can only imagine and see the end result in our mind. See what you want in high resolution. The world must manifest whatever your mind holds as constant.

Your Powerful Thoughts

Our ancestors were people of chosen words. They believed that the spoken word was powerful because it expressed the unseen power of the Creator which could become manifested in material form. The words you speak are very powerful, yet they are still only a limited representation of the thoughts they attempt to express.

Fear, doubt and insecurity can cause you to lose faith in your abilities, but beyond fear lays the unaltered potential of the mind. If your mind is the freedom train which will deliver you from bondage, then "you" are sitting in the conductor's chair. Your mind has boundless creative energy and it has the power to construct according to your direction and will. For that reason, your constructive power must be thoughtfully guided and directed. Be constantly vigilant and present to the choices you make with each second of your life. Just as you can harness this constructive power, your thoughts can equally hold destructive power if allowed to run like a wild bull. Your behavior simply responds to the direction given by your thoughts.

Without discipline, the greatness of your potential is often trapped among all of the pain and suffering you've endured. When this pain is unresolved, it bumps around in your mind as destructive and harmful thoughts. These destructive patterns of thinking cause a great deal of noise and disorganization. Just as you are unable to move around in a crowded house, your thoughts cannot find the room to foster new and positive ideas. Without the room they need to grow and prosper, your thoughts become scattered and random. This is how you keep yourself from optimal growth. The power to exercise control and mastery over your life is contained within the peace and stillness of your own mind. You must get past the fears, the hurts and the insecurities that haunt your darkest moments. Doubt and fear represent thoughts of uncertainty which rob you of creative, constructive energies. When you are frightened about your future or are anxious about your past, your mind races with thoughts of dread and remorse. The more importance you give to your fears, the greater significance they will have over your life.

We do so much to avoid suffering, and in denying our suffering, we forget that pain can also be a good teacher. Pain and suffering don't have to be a regular part of life, but both occur when we fail to appreciate that a greater mind is holding all things constant. There is no way that we can go through this life and not experience some sort of pain. Pain also has a healthy, adaptive purpose. Pain can teach you to locate what is wrong and draw attention to that problem area in order to resolve the root cause of the pain. Pain reminds you that the world is a place of constant transitions and change. Pain often occurs when you hold on and fail to accept the natural and intelligent flow of life. Pain can increase our tolerance and make us stronger, even healthier. Pain can teach us the importance of detachment.

What is detachment? It is learning a healthy distance between your higher sense of awareness and the emotional experience or reaction you might have. If you are overly identified with pain or any other emotion, you can be dragged right along with the experience and fail to maintain your center. When do you know that you have obtained an ability to detach? When you are willing to let go of your expectations; when you are willing to go along for the ride, for the shear excitement of the journey; when you accept life as it is, then you have obtained a level of detachment.

Some people are overly identified with their pain. They hold on to it like a blanket and only have an identity that is based on the pain they've endured. The pain you have endured does not and should not define the person you are; rather it should fortify your character and spirit. There is a sacred power located at your core which is there to transform all suffering and all pain into peace and tranquility. When you suffer, when you experience deep pain, it is because you are holding some notion of the way you believe things should have been. In your mind's eye, you are convinced you know all there is to know. Your disappointment creates hurt and suffering. The more pain and suffering you experience, the tighter you tend to hold on to your notion of the way things ought to be. In your rigidity, you fail to be present to the possibilities of the moment. In your fear of letting go, you restrict the possibilities that something greater than what you could have ever imagined could be waiting for you.

Watch what you think! Hold constant guard over your thoughts. Your mind is fertile ground. Whatever seeds you plant are the seeds you will come to harvest. Your mind knows only to multiply those thoughts you allow to take root. If most of your time is spent thinking about all the bad things that have happened to you, you will see evidence of mistreatment all around you. Thoughts reproduce and become manifested in your body as energy and behavior. You have a right to live your life as you best see fit. You can either choose to believe that you are an active participant in the creation of the life you live, or you can believe that the cards are stacked against you and that you will be eternally oppressed by people and forces around you. There is ample evidence to prove each one of these views as correct. Whichever view becomes your truth depends on the evidence you gather. The world responds to your attention. The world is simply a field of potential and unlimited possibilities. It is your focused or un-focused attention that makes your world.

When you were a child, you learned to protect yourself from pain and you guarded yourself from fear. Over time, you developed a specific way and style of reacting to the world. These ways of coping and reacting become automatic and are hard-wired to your brain. This means that you have the tendency to react the same way over and over, even before you are able to assess whether the situation is appropriate to your reaction. Children who hold their breath to get what they want may become adults who feel personally injured when they can't get others to do as they wish. Some adaptive techniques which worked when you were younger don't quite work the same way when you are older. The rigid adult may say, "If you really loved me you would do and say everything I want you to do and say." Having such expectations is damaging to your development and keeps you from obtaining growth and maturity. Learn to move with the rhythm of life. You must maintain a flexible mind in order to continue to grow. You can choose to make your life as rich or as impoverished as you dare imagine. This is the concept of free will and it is your birthright.

You can choose to be happy or you can even choose to live your life shrouded in resentments, pain and regret. You may ask yourself, "Who in their right mind would choose not to be happy?" Everyone desires to be happy and free; but when our thinking becomes rigid, we don't allow the flow of life to show us the great potential of creation.

It is All in the Mind

The concept of a Creator exists, first and foremost, within the capacity of the mind to hold the omnipotent, boundless nature of the universal force, of which you are a perfect expression. The mind is the vehicle that will deliver you to freedom and joy. Understanding the regal nature of your past supports the legitimacy of your connection to the universe and to the Creator. By understanding the efforts and the significance of your native ancestors' contributions, you will be able to fully appreciate the power of the gift entrusted to you. These teachings have endured for hundreds of years and their message will transform your life by revealing all that you need to know to claim the happiness, health, love, joy and prosperity you so richly deserve. The key to unlocking your true potential, the key to your transformation, is imbedded in these teachings. Read carefully and decipher the clues from your ancestral past and witness how these clues empower your life. Stay open and receptive. This is the story of your life, but more importantly, it is the story of your transcendence from lack to abundance, from bondage to freedom, from pain to joy.

Our native psychology is deeply rooted in tradition and spirituality. Your ancestors saw each manifested life as an expression of the divine power of creation. The power of the Creator is present in all that you see and do. There is a force that cannot be contained by any man-made institution, no matter how powerful that institution pretends to be. Freedom and happiness are not only possible, but they are your divine right and destiny. Yet, you have internalized so many harmful myths about yourself, your world, your origin and your relationship to the divine. You can retrain your mind to believe the original truth that is still implanted at your core.

If you can stay still against the fears and the uncertainty that surround your life, you will hear the whisperings of strength and truth. Listen and honor that inner wisdom of your mind. In so doing, you will always discover the healing, ancestral source of all goodness and truth which is your authentic nature. If you can quiet your mind in your moments of uncertainty, you will always hear the voice of truth telling you, assuring you, that everything will be alright, that everything is alright right where you are! When you become capable of reaching moments of stillness and tranquility, no matter what appears to be happening around you, you will learn that there is no physical or material condition you cannot overcome.

Lesson: Listen to You

There is a voice within you that knows your truth. That "intuitive knowing" is inherent to you from your past. Along the way, you pick up messages that distort, block or suppress those original messages. At some point you forget the sound of your own voice and begin to live your life according to these false messages. You have been following blindly along, seldom questioning the mythical story you have internalized as your self identity. Why do you believe the things that you believe? Why do you continue to repeat to yourself so many negative messages about your worth? It is time for you to pay attention to the transmission of your thoughts. Become mindful. How?

Here's a brief exercise. Allow yourself to sit in silence for fifteen minutes a day. Disable phones and all of the demands of the world. Take a deep breath, hold it in, and release. Watch your breath enter and feel it leave your body. Focus on the air coming through and caressing your nostrils, and then feel your breath as it leaves your body through your lips. Try to keep your mind clear of thoughts. If a certain thought enters your mind, don't get upset with yourself. Recognize the thought and let it go. Get back to your goal of keeping your mind free of thought. At first, this simple exercise will seem difficult or even boring, but stay with it. Your mind requires some discipline to maintain a certain level of clarity.

Your thoughts are energy. Broken down to the smallest chemical components, your thoughts are a firing of neurons which create electrical charges in your brain. Break down your thoughts further and you come to see that your thoughts are comprised of the same invisible and indivisible sparks of energy that have created everything. The source and potential of your thoughts are unlimited and such source can be directed. Learn to stop the automatic negative thinking. Verbalize the negative thought. Give it a voice and give it words. Hear yourself repeat the negative thought and ask yourself if that is truly what you believe to be true? You will see that, most of the time, these negative thoughts are clearly irrational. As you confront the irrationality of your thoughts, you will catch yourself in moments of deepening self awareness and insight. The power of your thoughts manifests everything that is matter and material in your world. The world of your everyday life begins with the thoughts and the assumptions you hold in your powerful mind.

You become aware that you could be setting up barriers to the realization of your true potential. You may be the one and only person getting in the way of your happiness. Sometimes we want things to change, but we do not want to go through the actual discomfort or even excitement created by change. We want to be out of a bad relationship, but we have gotten so used to things just the way they are. We want success, but at the same time we don't think our bad luck will ever change. When you hold two contradicting thoughts or desires in your mind, you cancel out your potential for progress and growth. One thing cannot be true and false at the same time. Your mind cannot grant you two opposing requests. You cannot, for example, say you have a problem with your significant other when they lose their temper and then not say anything to them for fear of creating more conflict. By not saying something you are contributing, assuring that the mistreatment you claim you don't want will occur again. How much strain can you tolerate? A great deal! Your "tolerance" tends to increase with each exposure. You can create your own misery as much by doing things that are harmful to you as by not doing anything to stop harm from coming to you. There are endless examples of how we sabotage our own success and personal progress without self awareness. Showing up late to an interview, getting angry and retaliating against your boss, getting up late the morning of a big exam, are just some common ways your subconscious mind acts hidden myths of unworthiness.

You believe strongly that there must be clear and logical reasons why you haven't obtained the level of success and joy that you deserve. Yet, you are coming to the realization that anger, revenge and retaliation do not solve anyone's pain. There is no gain obtained in being angry or blaming others for a history of pain and suffering. It is a much greater challenge to learn to react to hatred with love, compassion and understanding. You understand that fighting an external enemy only creates internal division and strife. As all things begin with the power of a thought, you know there can be no such thing as an external enemy unless you conceive of one as such. Listen to your "gut" but do not react in anger or revenge. Take an extra moment and hold back your impulses. Learn to use the higher seat of consciousness which is at your core and react with understanding and compassion. If we truly are all connected and are all part of the same family, then it serves no purpose to be angry and resentful towards anyone. There is a universal law which acts the same for everyone. This universal law multiplies whatever thought "energy" it receives from your mind and acts upon that; regardless of whether the thought content is positive or negative, it will multiply. Depressive thoughts create more depressive thoughts while thoughts of hope, courage and faith also create more of the same. The universal laws operate consistently for everyone and cannot be bypassed by anyone.

Your ancestors believed that if the natural rhythm of life was disrupted, illness, confusion and chaos would take over. For this reason, it is wise not to get attached to strong emotions since everything is governed by the constant law of movement and change. In the midst of darkness, there is always light. In the midst of confusion, clarity tends to emerge.

Lesson: Life Can Be a Friendly Game

Consciousness and thought are the universal building blocks at the core of all creation. The connection that we have to this creative force is clear and direct. You can participate in the creation process and can direct that creative energy to fit your needs. Some of us have been confused by old manipulative messages we picked up along our path. Your individual pain, suffering and fear keep you blinded to the greater possibility for your life and thereby limit your access to your full potential. Your ancestors believed that change and movement are the force governing life; therefore, when bad times come, face them without judgment and see them as learning opportunities. Such experiences are placed in your path to teach a valuable lesson. You can approach the lesson with resentment and struggle or you can make the lessons of life a friendly and gentle game. You have generations of wise elders to draw upon for experience. When you recognize all the invisible arms that have supported and guided your journey thus far, you can reach back and claim the lessons of the elders.

The development of your mind and your consciousness represents the evolution of the collective thought for the entire human race. Your thinking and reasoning have evolved from the impulsive fight or flight reactions to the sophistication of critical reason, abstract thought and discernment. You are like a map to the past and a link to the future. In your mind and in your awareness there are benchmarks that guide your journey. These benchmarks allow you to move forward when you are ready or they keep you in a holding pattern until you have learned the lesson at hand. If you master the given benchmark, you advance to the next level. If you do not master the benchmark you simply stay right where you are until you are ready to advance to the next level. It's a friendly game, really! If you are seeing with the right vision, you can't help but recognize the signs wherever you look. On the other hand, anger, resentment, pain and sorrow can cause you to misperceive events and intentions. If you can't perceive your environment accurately, you may miss many friendly and helpful friends along the way. Regardless of how you approach your journey, do so lovingly. Be kind to yourself always and enjoy your unique and individual process and style of learning.

4

On the Path of Self Knowing

Life can often seem like a difficult load to carry. It is particularly difficult when your way of solving problems is still defined by the ways in which you have approached life in the past. So often, the wounds of the past create a scar. That hard tissue makes it difficult to stay open to the new lessons that life presents. Without self awareness, you are bound to repeat the same patterns and mistakes. Pain, trauma and abuse can leave such a mark in your life that your mind essentially freezes and tries to solve past problems as if they were taking place today. The mind often feels like a broken record as past wounds seem to constantly re-appear in different people and situations. You can feel yourself a victim and look to others for the love and rescuing you deserve. If you feel you need rescuing, you give someone else the power to decide whether you should be rescued or not. Keep in mind that no one has the same interest in your life that you do.

There is an additional trauma which is caused when you become divorced from your true identity. Cultural identity is a source of strength because it connects you to the past and because it provides a blue print to your potential. The collective stories of your ancestors still influence your personality, the way you love, the way you hurt and the way you see the world in general. Forcing yourself to fit into the perspectives and expectations of a different culture can often leave you feeling inferior, incapable and even crazy. With time, your unique gift and voice can seem to grow silent. It is easy to ignore your intuition and the power of your own sense of awareness. You begin to doubt yourself and fall into situations which do not serve your greater good. As you begin to pursue external definitions of success, your search can leave you exhausted and unfulfilled. How many jobs or promotions will it take for you to be satisfied with your life? Often, you might feel that this "self-improvement" stuff is nice, but not for you. You don't have time. You are too skeptical of empty promises that don't deliver. Find the core of your true self and you will discover the rich promise of the past just waiting for you to claim it. Sometimes it is tempting to turn your complicated life over to someone else so that they can manage your affairs and you can have a break. If you give someone else the power to control your life hoping they will make you happy, you will eventually end up feeling used, abused, abandoned and disappointed. It is never too late to take charge of your life. Getting back to the teachings of our ancestors can serve as a guide in achieving self knowledge, balance and harmony.

Life-Truth-Energy-Action
Tonalli

The ancestors believed that the source of all life is an indescribable power which flows through everything and is the essence of all things. This essence is called *tonalli* and it flows through all individuals, planets, animals, mountains -- in short, all of creation. *Tonalli* is the indescribable "stuff" which is imbued with wisdom and the code to realize the potential of all that it embodies. *Tonalli* is the spark of the Creator that becomes manifested in unique form. The Creator thus comes to reflect him/herself in all that is created. An acorn has a *tonalli* to become an oak tree. You have a uniqueness that has been imagined and was born in the infinite mind that created all the planets and stars. Everything and everyone therefore has a *tonalli* that seeks expression regardless of obstacles or barriers encountered. Your *tonalli* is your potential seeking realization and actualization.

The realization of your uniqueness makes you part of a larger reality. Through you the Creator chooses to become embodied, seeking individualized expression so as to demonstrate the infinite love and potential of creation. You have a *tonalli* which is very different than mine and everyone else's. The creator has designed your *tonalli* to fit perfectly into a universal plan imbued with infinite wisdom and love. *Tonalli* does not have a direct translation, but in modern terms, it is inclusive and synonymous with *life, energy, truth* and *action*. Perhaps by examining the ancestral connotation of these words we might come closer to understanding the original significance of *tonalli*.

Life

Life is the expression of energy in material form. It is indivisible and eternal. Life, in this case, is not a thing, but an ever evolving, eternally developing force which finds expression in the temporal physical manifestation. Life is perpetual motion, expressing itself through our limited understanding of each moment to moment as it unfolds within our consciousness. Every present moment is filled with immeasurable potential, but you must be able to recognize it as such. If you are like most people, too often you tend to spend much of your life obsessing about what is wrong and what is lacking and you fail to appreciate the perfection and simplicity of each moment just as it is. In your limited ability to see beyond the confines of your individual reality, you are often unable to see that it is not the moment that is faulty, but your judgment and perception about the moment. Your fear and resistance, your desire to control, manipulate and anticipate every next step, forces you to become anxious with hesitation. You need a certain assurance to move forward and you attempt to convince yourself that you can control whatever happens next. The hurts and the pains that you've endured make you question and doubt the intelligence of the Creator. You start to doubt that all which transpires is truly designed by a loving power with your best interest in mind.

You recall vividly every person that brought you to your current state of confusion and you believe that they are still out there, plotting and planning your demise. Life cannot flow through you if you are blocking yourself from feeling and experiencing what is new. You don't trust yourself and you question your potential, so you tell yourself that the reason why you don't advance is because others are out to get you. That is simply not the case. Most people are too concerned about their own life and their own craziness to think too much about anything else.

Life is a patient and abundant field of experience and we are all self-taught. Life unfolds and offers its gifts to you at the rate in which you are able to decode and process its language. There is little you can do to stop this flow. Your resistance will only make the force of life find an alternate route of expression. A person standing defiantly against the currents of a river finds a river moving through and around. At best, the current will move around your resistance; at worst, you will be swept away by the force of the river. Life will always find a way to produce itself in perfect harmony even out of the greatest confusion and chaos.

Fear will cause you to resist; but if you can control your tendency to react impulsively, you will be able to unify your strength and will with the very force of life. When you are able to let go, you will discover that the force of life responds to your will. Find the serenity to move with the current of life and let it carry you to your intended destination. If you struggle, bemoaning why you were not born rich, or why your parents treated you so badly, you will not be able to move away from that place of lack and hurt. If you are punishing yourself for things that you did years ago, there is really nothing that you can do to change that past, nor is there anyone that can free you from your personal prison other than yourself. Life will continue to flow despite your resistance. You must resign yourself and accept that powerful force which is intelligence. Life knows what to do at every perfect moment. If you are able to trust and move with the divine intelligence of life, then you can use the force of life to favor your circumstances. Prepare yourself for your greater tomorrow by taking the first step in faith and acceptance.

Our native ancestors understood that an individual life is the same as the universal life which is expressed through everyone and everything. Life is therefore eternal. Human life is the embodiment, the incarnation of the divine creative force, which is forever present, complete and whole. Life is a force that eternally regenerates itself with and through love. Our native ancestors believed that death is an illusion, a great myth. They believed that when your physical body stops functioning, your *tonalli* and mind survive without material form. You remain aware of universal forces and are able to rely on different sensory preceptors than your physical senses. Your mind joins the collective mind of the universe to co-create for eternity. Know that you are in safe hands and that you will always be greeted and guided by others who have gone and carved the path before you.

Energy

Energy is that vibration and charge that is created by action in motion. Energy, like the other great truths of creation, is also eternal. Energy expands outward, forever impacting change through motion and contact. While energy is inexhaustible, our physical bodies are limited by time and space. It is your body that becomes exhausted. It is your thoughts of fear and limitation which leave you feeling tired and worn out. When you feel worn out, remember your source. Energy is abundant and ever present. You can have access to this boundless energy if you maintain your body and your thoughts connected to the source of this energy.

Sometimes, grabbing at everything becomes a means to avoid investing energies specifically where they are most required. This is a reaction manifested in fear of missing the opportunities for joy or as a means of not having to prove your true potential. When you reach for everything that comes your way and you fail to grasp anything, you can feel incapable of success. You can always tell yourself you were never really committed to try your best. Soon you find yourself exhausted and burned out.

Energy works best when your thoughts focus specifically on an intended route. Energy can have the power to transform anything if it is applied with intention. Practice those activities which will generate a positive amount of energy. If you sit in front of the television set for too long, you are likely to find yourself feeling tired and depressed. If energy does not have a vehicle to flow through, the results are lethargy. A great deal of energy is also expanded by the consumption of drugs or alcohol. When you consume substances in large quantities, the delicate balance of your body becomes disturbed and it takes a great deal of your energy to have your body recover its delicate equilibrium.

Energy generates more of its kind; positive energy attracts more positive energy and negative energy generates more of the same. Thoughts are energy too. Positive energy can leave you feeling refreshed and renewed. Negative energy can leave you feeling beaten and exhausted. When you begin to think of what is wrong in your life, you can easily begin to generate suffering and remember everything else that has ever gone wrong.

Truth

Tonatiuh sees all. The central eye of the Fifth Sun governs all. Everything that exists is within the awareness of the One mind. Sometimes you can lie to yourself and others, but no one can escape the universal intelligence that penetrates through any lie and false perception. According to the native ancestral teachings, because your life is a reflection of the one life of the Creator, within your life there is the potential to delve deeply into the eternal waters of truth. Truth is the one search that most unifies your mind with the mind of the Creator. The search and dedication to truth allows you to be in, participate and share with the eternal mind of the Creator. Truth speaks an intuitive language and is apparent in all you see and all you experience.

Along with the divine gift of life, you were also given the opportunity to utilize your own ability to employ "free will". You can, in other words, stare truth in the face and still choose to turn your back on what you know. The actions and consequences of your choice are not sin. There is no divine score keeper or referee keeping a tally of your choices and actions. You will come to know the results of your actions by the resulting reactions. Experience will be your teacher. The path of truth, while it may be the most obvious, is also the most demanding. Many people know what is right and true, but dilute themselves because of personal power, pride and arrogance. They can tell themselves that there is no such thing as truth or "doing the right thing", but experience will eventually teach them otherwise.

Most of us know intellectually that all human beings are "created equal" as the United States Constitution declares. That you and I are "endowed by (our) Creator with certain inalienable Rights..." Yet hoarding of power and material wealth has been integrated into our social and political life. In our society, certain privileges are assigned based on the diluted notion that people have varying degrees of worth. How else can we explain hatred in all its shapes and forms? War, racism, homophobia, immigrant hatred, and the ruthlessness of economic domination are forces that remain in our society based on the distorted belief that the Creator distributed power in varying degrees according to people's varying worthiness. The life of every human being has equal validity in the eyes of the Creator even if society attempts to distort that truth. Any form of mistreatment based on a notion of inequality of individuals is a human-made illusion.

Truth is the force which shapes the content of our lives. The voice at your central core is directly connected to the source of divine intelligence and truth. That intuitive knowing is connected to the ancestral past. The voice of truth never leaves you. You decide that it sometimes is not convenient or desirable to hear its whispers. When you are plagued by self doubt and feelings of inadequacy, you may feel that the voice of truth has abandoned you because you are not worthy. Whether you consider yourself worthy or not is of small consequence and significance. Your worth has been determined by the source of infinite wisdom. You have been "thought" and "created" into existence by the self knowingness of an intelligence that governs all of creation.

Truth does not bind you to live a boring and uneventful life. It points to the freedom inherent in your nature. It is your search for a full life which leads you to seek truth. It is the knowing of truth which sets you free from the binding hold of temporary and transitory illusion of pleasure, possession and power. The search for the truth is the engine that drives your life. Truth is that inner voice of freedom which promises a rich and fulfilling life beyond what you thought possible. Truth is instantaneous and ever present. Whenever you find yourself lost and confused, sit in silence and listen to your inner truth. While you may not see the entire road ahead, you will, most assuredly, see the next step. Learn to clear your mind of any thought and hear beyond sound. See beyond sight. Listen to the wisdom of emptiness and listen to the truth contained in the silence. In moments of perfect stillness you can come to experience the universal truth contained within every passing moment.

Action

Everything in life is in a perpetual state of change and fluctuation. Action, movement and motion represent another universal law. Every living thing is in a constant state of motion and change. Even the most solid of mountains is forever impacted by the force of action. You can resist the universal responsibility of action with non-action, but even the decision to stand still in the face of constant change is action. Action creates a momentum which in turn creates patterns and uniformity. You are often pulled by the actions of the many. You can be pulled to follow the pack and live much of your life in uniformity of what you observe around you. At times, a voice deep inside you requests that you listen and take action in a manner that might be different than the actions taken by the many. It is certainly much easier to move along the beaten path carved by the herd, but it is the "road less traveled" which often leads to greater understanding by increasing the boundaries of your comfort zone. There is a unique force inside you which drives you to act as you believe. There is a message within you that only you can express to the world. How you act influences your individual life as much as it influences the life of all those around you.

The choices you make create patterns of behavior which set chains of events into action. These reactions often have irreversible consequences. You may think you have free will to do as you please, but free will is irrelevant if you constantly act and choose only that which is familiar and comfortable to you. Acting in the same fashion always will always give you the same results.

Action requires a constant willingness to forego the comforts of the familiar for the promise of growth and self awareness. Action is the natural state of the universe and it is the natural rhythm of life. Action is the fuel that propels creation. Action is an interaction of forces waiting for you to choose among the infinite number of possibilities laid before you. Your actions create a chain reaction which reverberates upon the fabric of creation. Like a pebble dropped in a still pond, the outgoing waves echo the fall of the pebble long after it falls to the bottom. Be aware of your actions; follow the rings they create as they impact others. Always choose to act with self awareness.

Your Life Script

Myths have the power to inform and transform your life. By acting as cultural templates, the myths of a society serve as a framework for the development and understanding of culture and behavior. You may not be immediately aware that the person you are, what you call your "self", is made up of countless stories you have heard and combined into the story you have created for yourself. Some of these stories are legends of old ancestors. Other stories are memories from the movies and shows which have shaped your views on any given subject. Other memories you hold are stories you have heard from friends and family members but which you don't really personally recall. Your personality is made up of the messages you take away from these stories and the manner in which you personally interpret and make sense of the themes in such stories. Because you are a product of a collision of two distinct world cultures, you tend not to see your complete story depicted in the history books or in the psychology texts. These books tend to outline the nature and teachings of Western influence on your development. Western myths tell only half of your story. The ancient voices of the *Nican Tlaca*, of Aztec heroes, gods and rulers, seldom make their way into your collective consciousness to inform your life script.

Early on, we are taught that everyone has the same chances at success and achievement. Sooner or later you may learn that no matter how hard you work at fitting in, you will feel a failure because you are trying to fit into a model of life that does not represent your reality. It is easy then to feel out of place and to develop anger and resentment. You follow a path set before you which has really been designed for those who have authority and power. You wish to be included as an equal, but you struggle with the realization that society sets different values and expectations on individuals based on race, gender, color of skin, earning capacity and access to power. You feel like the least popular child in school, rejected by all the cool kids who will never see you as one of their own. It is hard to turn away from the majority's expectation without feeling a failure, but you must discover what makes you an individual and move away from the pack. The object of this game called life is to find your specific talent and your unique flavor and then share your gift with the world. When your individual light shines brightly, everyone else will be drawn to you. Don't seek external power and inclusion; seek these traits within yourself first.

Your Self Worth

It is easy to forget what you are truly worth and who you really are. There are so many things in your heart and mind and you simply cannot find the words to express all that is inside of you. Bombarded by chaos and false images of poverty, violence and lack, you focus on surviving and might have never had the experience of learning the important language of emotions. You might have never been allowed to speak about your feelings and so now, when you feel it essential to communicate your thoughts, you don't know how to do so. When you can't express how you feel, you act out what cannot be communicated with words. How can you express what is in your heart, what is your central truth, when you don't feel you have the language necessary? Often words are hard because they reveal clues to complex injuries you feel are better left untouched. You don't lack anything at all, least of all self awareness. What is often missing is the faith in knowing that the past suffering can disappear completely and liberate necessary energy for further development.

Wanting recognition, validation and love are basic human desires, essential for healthy development. So often your environment has not been able to provide you with even these most essential of human needs. It is difficult to give yourself love and acceptance if you have seldom experienced genuine love from others in your life. As an adult, you are expected to love yourself and to give yourself all the praise you need; but if you have heard constant messages that you are not worthy, it is difficult to go against what you have been taught. External validation, hearing from others that you are worthy of love, is important particularly during your childhood. From this early validation, you develop into an adult with an internal awareness as one who is worthy of love. If you are still looking for external validation and confirmation of your worth, you are expressing a void that is deep and old. The child within you is still waiting for that love and approval to come from the adults who most mattered to you; yet the adults have grown old while you waited for them to express their love for you. You can wait an eternity and wish that the past was somehow different, but wishing for a better past cannot alter the reality of what is. You cannot change your past, but you can certainly impact your emotions about it.

Deep inside, you feel as though someone should be outraged at your past mistreatment. Some deep part of you cannot understand how the world goes on as if everything is alright, while you have been hurting for so long. You are absolutely right! Someone should have objected to your mistreatment. Someone should have recognized you were hurting and given you the unconditional love you so deserve; yet constantly looking backwards, waiting around for someone to set the record right, won't bring you the happiness you seek. You have to recognize that the manner in which you learned to interact with others and with your surroundings might not have been the optimum environment in which to thrive. Knowing that, there is a need to relearn love and acceptance, starting with you. You must reach that point in your awareness when you are able to connect to your past to recall the purity of your essence and the magnificence of your true identity. If you rely on any person other than yourself for confirmation of your self worth, you leave yourself vulnerable to their criticism, their conditional approval, their withdrawal and their devaluation of your worth. The only valid confirmation of your worth must come from the unfailing core within, which is never changing and always pure.

Life, Energy, Truth and Action are universal laws which operate indiscriminately and impersonally. Learn to act in accordance with these laws and the laws will act in your favor. Ignore the natural rhythm of these universal principles and you will be struggling against the very force of creation. Discover your *tonalli* and commit your life to realizing your full potential. Harmony and balance are also universal laws. Even chaos and discord eventually gravitate towards homeostasis. The universe functions because all is in balance with everything else. The planets and stars behave according to universal laws that govern their movement. You, as a part of this universe, are also governed by these same laws.

In order for you to play the part the universe intends for you, you must also be in balance and in harmony with these universal forces and principles. When you are out of balance you will inevitably experience disease. To reestablish health and happiness, you must first identify whatever is out of balance in your life and then, with courage and conviction, you must move to restore your sense of harmony. Your true potential lies in understanding your true origin and in knowing there are universal laws which can be applied to create the life you imagine. Dare to look beyond your perceived limitations and dare to stretch your mind beyond what you have told yourself is possible.

Taking good care of yourself is a revolutionary act because self care can alter the nature of the world you inhabit. In the larger view of life and the wisdom of the universe, there is no oppressor and there are no oppressed. There is only one life. When you feel that others are bent on treating you as though you are inferior, do not bother defending yourself or trying to prove them wrong. In your mind, simply hold the truth firmly and be patient. In time, the truth will make itself known. Eliminate any thought of inadequacy. Remind yourself that those who are aggressive towards you or seek to minimize your worth are simply confused and unaware of your truth. Don't engage them. To engage and confront individuals who are disinterested or distorted is to participate in the very distortion of reality. Maintain your hold on the truth as you understand it and the world will react accordingly.

As a student of karate, I have learned that no enemy will pick a fight with you unless they feel they have the power to beat you. It is not cowardice to choose not to engage an opponent that is bigger or stronger than you; it is simply a smart survival technique. This is a time when you must show respect and not defiance. Respect for those that might mean you harm will allow you time and space to observe their actions and interactions so that you can better choose how, when and whether you should engage. Learn to see the actions of those you perceive to be your enemies as your responsibility. You should not concern yourself with what someone else is doing to you, but rather what you can do to improve the situation. Remember that you are like a mirror held up to the face of the world around you. If someone becomes angry and hostile towards you, you can reach beyond your personal pain and anguish and alter the situation, but only if you don't internalize the other's behavior. It takes a much stronger and wiser person not walk into the traps of rage. Divert your attention elsewhere and do not engage. See the person who is aggravating you as a confused and insecure individual. See the person as someone who does not have the appropriate resources to adequately deal with the situation at hand. You have a choice as to how you will react to any given situation. The manner in which you react defines who you are.

Integrating a New Culture: A Balancing Act

We are only now beginning to understand the true impact on children and adults caused by migration. It is traumatic to leave your homeland and start a brand new life in a place where you are not accepted and you feel that you don't belong. It is most traumatic to start part of your life in one culture, believing the world to be a certain way and then start again by unlearning everything you previously held as reality. How can you tell yourself that all you learned is inaccurate and even inferior to what everybody else considers to be valid and real? How do you continue to emphasize the importance of maintaining pride and identification with your culture of origin? If you don't maintain a connection to your culture, who do you become? Cultures are models through which reality is interpreted. Children who develop with a solid sense of safety and belonging and are rooted in tradition will have a greater ability to master their surroundings with confidence.

If you doubt the value of your cultural heritage you may begin to feel uncertain. Many people report feeling depressed, lonely and lost as they try on identities that are not their own. If you are hesitant about embracing your cultural origins, you will be more vulnerable to the opinions of critics. You have survived all of these years and have learned to adapt to your demanding environment by working at jobs that require all of your physical energies and leave you emotionally spent. Be certain you don't lose sight of what and why you work. Images of material possessions, sex and the good life fill your head with ideas that somehow there is a better life somewhere else other than where you are. These images say you would be happier if only you had more things, more power and more of everything. Yet, the more you chase these things the more you become a slave to the chase and the desire. You begin to internalize images of an identity not your own, trying to be something you are not as you try to rise above what you perceive to be your miserable situation.

The increasingly long and demanding hours you spend at work seem to be just sufficient enough to keep hunger at bay. It seems that no matter how hard you work you cannot get ahead. No matter how hard you try you cannot get to where you once dreamed you could go. Have you given up on your dream? Have you become content to work at a job you hate, telling yourself that at least you have enough to pay the bills? Certainly you are meant to live a fuller and richer life, but you have to believe that living such a life is possible regardless of the circumstances presently surrounding you.

You want to change your life, to move beyond the point of always feeling you are lacking. You want to get to the point where you are manifesting abundance, which is the natural order of the universe. But how can you manifest abundance when it seems you are always in crisis management mode? You determine that you must work harder and longer in order to provide for others all that you never had. You build resentment directed towards the world, but mostly, this resentment is often directed towards yourself. You find yourself trapped in the eternal treadmill, running faster and harder, just to stay one step ahead. Your children grow fast and you are seldom around. While you are busy providing and working to secure their future, the present slips through your fingers. One day your children may say that you gave them all the material things they could have hoped for, but they will tell others they would have traded it all for a bit more of your time and a bit more of an opportunity to know you better. No child ever says, "I spent too much time with my father or with my mother."

The challenge of our time is making freedom and evolution possible within the reality in which we live. You affirm that you don't have time or money, or that circumstances in your life are unique and hopeless and that this "self-help" material does not relate to you. You are affirming the life that you don't want. By focusing on what you don't have and what is not working, you reinforce the negative and it becomes more real. No matter how chaotic things might seem, you must find the time to be still and clear your mind. Sit in silence and listen to the truth. Learn to still your mind and reconnect with the infinite power of creation at your core.

You are the Writer of Your Life Story

How aware are you of your story and the personal myths which you have adopted as your life script? Write down your life story or tell it to a friend or into a tape recorder and play it back to yourself. You will begin to recognize that certain themes keep repeating. You will hear certain explanations and rationalizations you offer to explain why you are where you are and not where you want to be. You are likely to attribute your faults and shortcomings on others you feel have blocked you from your good.

Make a list of your injuries and past hurts and of those individuals you hold accountable. How many people do you still hold accountable? How and why did they hurt you? When you were a child you were unable to defend yourself, but today you are an adult with freedom to choose. Why have you not been able to forgive? Your parents, past lovers, past bosses, the list of the many who have come in and out of your life could be quite lengthy; yet, despite all the hurt and pain you've endured, no one person has power over your life unless you willingly allow them that power. How you react to people and events around you is purely and completely within your power and your decision.

If you are aware of the script that is directing your behavior, you are more likely to exercise control over your thoughts. Uncover the held assumptions which organize your life. You will find that these held assumptions are often left over from the perspective of an injured child. These assumptions often no longer apply to the world you inhabit. You can then alter the script to better fit your life and your desired outcome.

Your life is like a beautiful book bound in the finest leather and silk, but with all the remaining pages still to be written upon. You are not only the main character in this story, but you are also the co-creator. What do you want your life story to be? Is your life story a celebration or a lamentation? If your story is a lamentation, you might receive pity and sorry glances. You might even find someone to show you a bit of kindness for a while; but sooner or later, stories of lament, suffering and pain tend to depress you and depress the people around you. You might say you cannot help feeling down, but the people around you may simply decide to not come around you anymore because you tend to be a downer. Sooner or later, you will look around and find there is no one interested in sharing the lamenting story with you.

One of the noble truths in Buddhism is that in life there is suffering; but how we react to suffering can determine whether we grow or stagnate. Many times, when suffering enters your life, you react impulsively by creating barriers and walls to keep you from your pain. You feel these barriers will protect you from further hurt, but such barriers will keep your pain blocked inside and will keep others from connecting with you.

Rather than taking the opportunity to re-evaluate the significance of the painful experience, you shut down to the pain. Moreover, rather than evaluating the efficacy of your thoughts and your chosen direction in life, you hold on even more firmly to the idea that the world is a place of sadness and suffering as evidenced by the lack of people around you. These thoughts reinforce your reality, assuring that the experience will be repeated. If your current life story is one of lamentation, you need to ask yourself what this story needs in order for it to turn into a story of celebration. If you are suffering because you were abused, then forgive the abuser and move on. If you are suffering because you are oppressed, then take charge. Speak up and do something to change your situation. Make a commitment to move away from the comforts of the past.

If you turn your story into a tale of celebration, you will begin to attract more positive experiences to you. You will attract more of what you desire because when you are able to celebrate the life you have; the energy that comes from you cannot help but infect everyone around you. Just as when you are depressed you repel, when you are joyous and grateful, you attract people who want the very same joy you have to be manifested in their own lives. This is not to say that you should ignore your pain and suffering, quite the contrary; amidst the receptive experience of your pain and suffering lays the key to your freedom and happiness. You must pay attention to the message of your pain and suffering while taking care to not become fascinated and absorbed by being in pain.

Lesson: Take Time

Taking time out of every day to sit quietly with your thoughts can be the best preventive medicine against any physical or mental illness. This is a society of individuals and high-achievers, competition and the endless pursuits of success. How much you are worth as a person can become how much you have achieved in life, or how much you earn. The race to the top can leave you exhausted and lost. There comes a time when you identify more with external evidence of achievement and less with the central core of your true worth. You are not your job and you are not your salary or achievements. You are so much more than that. The noise of life, the chaos of constant activity, can be deafening. You must take time for yourself. It doesn't matter if you only have ten minutes a day, but take the time to separate yourself from family, work, relationships and reconnect to your inner self.

A few months ago, I met Leticia at a women's conference. I noticed her in the crowd because she sat with her arms crossed and a sour look on her face the entire time I spoke. When I was finished with the presentation, Leticia rushed up to me and said angrily, "I thought your talk was very nice, but it is not practical or realistic. I am going through a divorce. My husband is an alcoholic and I just found out he's been cheating on me for years. My only son has been diagnosed as schizophrenic and is taking heavy medications. I have to take him to all of his appointments and keep him from killing himself. I have started taking antidepressants and sleeping pills and I feel I am going to lose my mind. How can I possibly take time for myself?"

Leticia feels that she is trying to do everything for everyone but herself. The fear and anxiety that comes from identifying with the events of her life have robbed her of her ability to care for herself. Her son becomes more afraid and feels helpless that he is not able to be strong and responsible for his mother during these tough times. Leticia feels her husband has taken her happiness and joy. Somewhere, Leticia lost herself to this pain and suffering. She feels that she must run and do everything in order to keep up with all of the pain and suffering. In reality, her increased activity will only add tension and stress. Ironically, she must let go of all the apparent crises and reclaim herself. Take time out to meditate, exercise, walk and play and to do the things that bring you pleasure. Find your joy again and you will be better able to care for yourself and others.

Lesson: Listen to Feedback and Know Your Values

On a very practical level, being familiar with your culture's teachings can help you stay sane. The world of today is diverse and multicultural. In order to thrive, you must be receptive to new experiences and learn to adapt to the ever evolving world. You cannot avoid having close intimate or professional relationships with others who grew up in cultures and backgrounds different than your own. Most arguments are really misunderstandings based on assumed values and ideals which we believe the other shares but which are never really "checked-out". Relationships play themselves out under the assumption that the other person believes what you believe and shares the same ideals and principles you do. In reality, you relate to people from your own unverified assumptions and views about life. Other people also relate to you out of their assumptions and cultural values. Seldom do we check out what we mean or wish to express to the other.

Love, freedom, commitment, passion, success and happiness are mere words that don't describe the extent and the richness of our understanding nor can these words fully reveal the depth of our thoughts. Words are symbols that attempt to describe the depth of our experience. When you encounter a disagreement with someone else, don't first assume you are wrong, nor insist that you are right. Take into consideration that you and the other person might actually be expressing two different world views which are equally valid and each in turn is defined by culture, traditions and the conscious and subconscious values that have been entrusted by past generations. Others will try to insist that their view is correct, perhaps because it is the majority perspective. Before you give in, examine your values and ideals. Understand what your parents and ancestors have taught you. Their teaching was honorable and was intended to make you happy. Honor their history by attempting to understand the value of their teachings and then decide where and how you should move forward. With such mindset, you will be able to determine where you should give in, where you should insist and where you must compromise.

Maria and Peter have been dating for five years and have recently decided to become engaged. Not long after they announced their engagement, they got into a huge argument and broke their commitment. Maria is a first generation Mexican-American with parents who have worked in factories all of their lives. Peter is Caucasian; his mother is a teacher and his father a police officer. His family espouses middle class values which include hard work and individuality.

Maria is frustrated because she feels that she has placed Peter in the center of her life and feels that Peter constantly rejects and ignores her. Peter feels that Maria's love is suffocating him and that it is too "heavy". He states that Maria seems to resent his work, while Maria states that she simply wants to feel that she matters to Peter. Maria's concept of love is based on lessons her parents taught her on how to be a woman and a wife. These values are not wrong, but they are not values necessarily shared by Peter. Peter's values are influenced by a drive to achieve and succeed. He feels that his wife should be supportive of his work and should recognize that he is happy doing what he loves to do. In order to move forward, Maria and Peter must come to a common definition and understanding of what they mean by love, commitment and companionship. They must reach some compromise which is respective and inclusive of each other's perspective.

So much of our society operates on trying to force one view, one perspective of life, as dominant and right. That type of thinking has caused so many wars and so much misery. Our ancestors' perspective of life, creation and the universe is very different than the dominant culture's perspective, but it is equally valid and can teach us all great lessons. Every person's world view includes their unique background and a perspective which is shaped by their ancestry and their heritage. People of different racial and ethnic backgrounds are influenced by the ideals and values taught to them by their cultures. With such divergent perspectives in life, it is a wonder we communicate and relate to each other at all!

In a diverse world, an open, non judgmental stance will always give you a broader, richer perspective. Listen to feedback that others give you with an open heart. Remember that others are your mirror. They are showing a reflection of yourself which may be out of your view, but which, with understanding and tolerance, will increase the boundaries of your imagination and open unexplored regions of consciousness. With an open heart, you can determine whether the feedback you receive fits your worldview or whether it is a perspective that comes from others' perception. If you listen with an open heart, you can decide when, where and how to compromise without buying into the myth of your inferiority. The lessons and values that come from ancestral teachings are anchors of the soul.

5

Time for Change

We are witnessing the greatest and most rapid changes the world has ever encountered. In this new environment, it is often hard to hold on to our traditions and to the richness of our past, particularly when we see the world forever altered with every passing moment. Time, space and distance have become less relevant concepts. The world has shrunk with the internet and with constant improvements in telecommunications, a dominant global market and affordable world travel. Our present economic woes often cause us to live in constant fear of tomorrow and to mistrust our neighbors. Large corporations have often merged with governments, creating a global culture where "right" and "might" are controlled by the rich and powerful few. Today, the effects of global warming are reported by the news media on a daily basis and with war, droughts, freezes and floods, we face the shortage of produce, oil and natural resources in every part of the planet.

Although we are more informed, we are also more isolated, anxious, fearful and depressed than ever before. Displaced by a largely unregulated global economy, the immigrant is forced to abandon the homeland in search of food and basic survival and is met with hatred and resentment. In many cities across our country, more than half of all Latino and African-American students are unable to complete a high-school education before dropping out. Our jails have become warehouses for the institutionalized and are often little more than training grounds for a life of more serious crime.

This is indeed a time for change! On a personal level we must each come to the realization that we can no longer afford to live a life of fear, frozen amidst the pain and anguish of our troubled past. You and I must give way to the eternally generous and ever forgiving heart that beats within us. This is the ancestral legacy, the eternal hope that ever holds firm to the true capacity of the human spirit. Your happiness is not only possible, but it is the logical outcome that results from living life more aware and liberated from the past. It takes a strong and decisive will to move away from fear, lack and pain. It takes an open and receptive mind to see that pain and suffering are temporary conditions. It takes a heart willing to exchange the comfortable, familiar pain and suffering for a new life of forgiveness and receptivity.

Every event in your life has been carefully orchestrated by the universal mind to teach you tolerance, acceptance, peace and serenity. Resist the natural rhythm of life and you will attract suffering and pain. As you become aware of your core beliefs, you increase your ability to see how these beliefs create the world you inhabit. Whatever and however you define your life, you will find that the universe is supportive and will always say "yes" to you. Are you a victim? Yes, if you believe you are. Are you poor and oppressed? Yes, if you believe that to be your truth. Are you about to change the world and embark upon the next evolutionary leap of consciousness and self realization? Yes, if you dare believe and if you dare let go of the limited understanding of life as you have lived it thus far. The challenge is to remain open and learn to see fear and pain as a friend and teacher. Don't shrink back! Move forward and let your pain and fear take you further than you have dared to go in the past. Move gracefully into the new land beyond the border of pain and fear. Expand the outer limits of your world. Let your mind entertain greater ideas than the ones you held yesterday.

The very purpose of your life on this planet is to boldly unfold a journey of self discovery. Just as the seventh wave of Huichilopotzli's children found the promised lands of Tenochtitlan, you can find the promised land of peace and self realization right where you are. Images of your heritage, like the Aztec Calendar and the eagle devouring the serpent, speak deeply to your psyche and can guide you along this journey. The eternal image of heaven and earth meeting in one place speaks as loudly today as it ever did. Etched on the surface of the Aztec Calendar, you will find the clues and support necessary to address the difficult moments in life.

The Force of Change

Ollin is the Aztec God of Change who devours everything material placed within its path. *Ollin* chews and spits out the physical remains of all living things, teaching us the pitfalls imbedded in becoming attached to an apparently solid but changing world. The mythical message of *Ollin* can provide certain reassurances in times when it seems nothing is going the way you anticipated. *Ollin* teaches that when change comes you do not need to panic.

There is a difference between incorporating change and simple awareness. Incorporating change means identifying with the emotions and meaning assigned to neutral and impersonal events as they happen. If you identify with these strong emotions, the force will pull you in and drag you down. Awareness implies feeling emotions and passions,

83

acknowledging their presence and impact, but recognizing such emotions as temporary and impersonal. You can allow yourself to experience pleasure and pain, but you maintain your center, recognizing their temporary existence.

The challenge is learning to let go of the need to control everything in life and to trust that we are being guided to realize our individually designed potential. The only thing you need to be concerned about is setting your intention. Don't focus on the things over which you hold no power to change, but be brave and courageous enough to change the things within your power. Do not hold on to your narrow vision of how you believe things are supposed to be. Don't hold on to the old ways of doing things simply because they give you comfort and are familiar. If you attempt to solve your old problems using the same tools and techniques you have always employed, you will repeatedly get the same results.

Tonatiuh, the God of Fire became the fifth and final Sun, the current Sun. *Tonatiuh* is the face that is carved in the center of the Aztec Calendar. His face looks out with reassurance, promising his children access to the transformative treasures. Within your mind is a field of infinite possibilities. In the Toltec and Aztec mythology, the *tonalli*, the energy of the soul can transform and take on any manifestation. Reality is an endless possibility of potential and your mind has the power to manifest infinite versions of reality. *Tonatiuh* teaches the simple lesson of standing still in order to hear the perfect peace already within you.

In times when life is governed by change, you must learn to keep moving with a strong conviction that you are being prepared for greater things. When *Ollin* governs, you must learn to purify your heart. Purification happens when you identify those thoughts that cause you suffering and you offer these up, asking the Creator to shine the light of truth on your false and limited perceptions. It is within the purification of your heart and mind that you are able to let go of the "lesser you", only to see and appreciate what and who you are becoming. During times of change, try not to hold on to any image of what or how you think your life should unfold, but keep a firm hold on your intention. Be confident in knowing all is working in divine order and in divine time. So many times, we work hard towards obtaining some goal, but in the process of obtaining that goal, we obsess over every detail and every little thing that could possibly go wrong. This obsession can bring negativity, fear, uncertainty and stagnation to our lives. Your dream might appear to be getting further away and you may work and struggle to keep it alive. What may seem like a step backwards might actually be a shift towards greater possibilities.

When change governs your life, it is a good day for transmutation. Transmutation is the process of transformation from the "less than" to the "greater than". Ancient Chinese culture teaches that crisis is also a moment of opportunity. Likewise, ancient native mythology teaches that the world and your own notion of "self" are concepts and ideas in constant transmutation, always becoming something better, always reaching for a higher form of existence. Allow your higher self to shine through in times of uncertainty and allow those forces of transmutation to guide you to the next stage of life. Deep change in your life may arrive like an earthquake, shaking your foundation and leaving behind a trail of ruin made up of the things you previously held as your truth. Such movement can leave you feeling as though you no longer know what to believe or what to affirm. When change comes, rationality, order, and our own preconceived notions, are tossed out the window. You must not be afraid of your own change. While the process of letting go may at first feel painful and awkward, trust that you are moving in the direct path of your happiness and bliss. Know that you are guided and protected. Embrace your transmutation with excitement and joy.

Remember that *Tonatiuh* was born as a result of sacrifice and personal transformation. *Tonatiuh's* face, in the center of the Aztec Calendar, shows his tongue sticking out. As you look at the central face closely, you see the tongue is in the form of a knife to symbolize *Tonatiuh's* transformation from sacrifice. *Tonatiuh* represents the central light of universal creation. His is the light that promises transformation and enlightenment in this lifetime. His is the same light that illuminates your mind, the same light that we've come to know as the Holy Spirit or the Light of the ONE. *Tonatiuh* rules as an ever present reminder of the capacity for self transformation imbedded in everyone. His face is not moved, not distorted, nor in any way distracted by the whirling and turning change of the four worlds that circle as they are consumed by change and destruction. *Tonatiuh* looks straight ahead, unaffected by the shape-shifters and the appearance of an ever changing world of material existence.

Our legends have foretold that one great day the curtain of appearances will fall away and we will come to experience the fullness of reality. Regardless of what world mythology or religion you use to organize your life, the path of the individual soul towards enlightenment, salvation, and the eventual reunification with the Creator, is the eventual path of each individual. In moments of transformation, when you are most consumed by the burning flames of the Fifth Sun, you may feel all alone. You may feel there is no hope left, no direction, and no friends who care. Know that during these times of pain, you are being prepared for something greater. You are being asked to let go of the painful past in order to make room for the great things about to arrive. Your mind and consciousness are ever expanding. Hold on to your dreams and your ultimate destination; you are closer than you think.

Avoid the Traps

Through the messages demonstrated within the collaborative relationship of the four creative forces of earth, wind, fire and water, you are able to appreciate the important message of personal balance and harmony. Balance and harmony allow for the prosperity of all life. Balance and harmony are guiding principles that govern growth and development. The harmony of life can be found as you keep the reins of your unbridled extremes in check. When anxiety, worry and despair take over your thoughts, it is difficult to step back and fight. During these times of stress and fear, it is difficult to find the strength to confront such thoughts and see them as the bandits and liars that they are.

Sometimes we worry and despair and we might secretly expect someone to come to our rescue and love that worry right out of our thoughts. Such an attitude of waiting places unfair burdens on you and the person who loves you. Your need to be rescued can become an incredible weight on the person who loves you because they are likely to feel incompetent and hopeless, ultimately knowing they can do nothing to save you. You must rationalize yourself into the truth.

Life is like a pendulum that swings back and forth. Sometimes, particularly when you are suffering, you may become overly fascinated by the thrill of seeking extreme forms of pleasure, just to feel alive. You may be consumed and become fascinated by the grueling pain of grief and sorrow; and in such despair, you may be tempted to wallow and stay there.

If you allow any one pleasure or any one loss in your life to dominate your thoughts, you simply become a subject to whatever strong experience controls you. When your pleasure becomes the thing that dominates your life, it stops being a pleasure and it becomes your master. Your emotions and your desires become your god. You are subjected to the highs that transport you out of your routine reality as much as you are subjected to the lows that keep you feeling hopeless and in constant despair. Without an anchor to the core of your truth, you start exploring peak experiences simply to escape your pain. Everything else that you might have previously considered important, such as family and relationships, takes a back seat. Your life becomes little more than the manifested evidence of that force, that desire or addiction that has come to consume your existence.

The Real Meaning of Sacrifice

When The Creator asked one of his four children to sacrifice himself for the birth of the Fifth Sun, it was the god representing humility and willpower who gave himself over in the sacrifice. By stepping into the fire, the son of the Creator became the Fifth Sun. *Tonatiuh* emerged as the triumphant Fifth Sun. While the son of the Creator believed he would die as a result of the sacrifice, he instead was transformed into something even greater than what he could have imagined.

The similarities of this Aztec myth to the story of Jesus Christ are strong and readily evident. Jesus prayed in the Garden of Gethsemane fearing what was to transpire. While hanging on the cross, in His darkest hour He believed His Father had abandoned Him. It was just past that second of fear and panic, and past that moment of death, that Jesus, the man, emerged victorious as the Eternal Son of God, resurrected and transformed into pure spirit, the pure light of a new and eternal being.

Even if you are not a religious person, you must appreciate the theme of personal transformation. Notice when you are faced with a great challenge, that in your darkest hour something shifts and you are lifted up, renewed and strengthened. It is as if you are transformed into someone greater, stronger, more resilient and more aware than the person you were before. What you sacrifice is fear, uncertainty, pain and suffering. These attachments are given away in sacrifice and in faith, knowing that the truth beyond appearance is the opposite of these seemingly solid attachments.

It is important to recognize and trust in that transformative value of sacrifice. Sacrifice the bad habits, the weight of suffering and held resentments, and learn to live in the moment. When you sacrifice something, the only thing that you ever really lose is your fear. Always, in the process of the sacrifice, as you give away that which you previously thought brought you comfort and security, you realize that you were actually trapped and controlled by those thoughts that kept you comfortable. The ritual of sacrifice is a transformation from the old self into a richer, fuller life. It is letting go of the lesser to open up to the greater. Sometimes the results of that transformation may not be readily apparent.

If you have ever lifted weights you have experienced the "burn", that painful feeling that results the day after your work-out. Your muscles react in pain, yet this pain is precisely what transforms and sculpts your muscles. Call this pain the sacrifice. The discipline that it takes to stay focused on your intention and your heart's desire will teach you to say no to certain distractions in order to stay on course. Sometimes you might have to say no to an extra slice of cake if you want to fit into your dress. Call this the sacrifice and say no with a glad heart that knows it is saying yes to a greater good. Know that you are always held by a power that wishes you goodness; a power that waits patiently for your decision to participate.

Our native ancestors understood the power of transformation. For our ancestors, the heavy emphasis on "the self" did not exist and they saw the individual life as a mere illusion. That is why our ancestors willingly walked into sacrifice. Like the example set by their god before, they set out to prove that death was nothing but an illusion of lack. When the individual is de-emphasized, the community is elevated. The meaning of the term "La Raza" does not refer to a race of people, but to the "mass" or "the collective". The term refers to the reverence of the community as a source of life and identity. The greatness of the Creator, the diversity of His beauty and power is better understood by contemplating the power, wisdom, and varied splendor of the family as a unit and system.

Our ancestors believed that the individual self was nowhere as important as the good of all. They in fact, believed that the experience of the individual self was often a trap that distorted reality, created illness and pathology. Everyone is celebrated as an individual and as a perfect and complete expression of the Creator, but the individual can only be understood through the contributions made to the community. In a belief system such as this, there is no fear of death. It was the ultimate honor for an ordinary person to become one with the Creator. The moment of their choosing was the moment of their transmutation. Through ritual an average person could see himself connected, celebrated, and prepared as the son of the eternal Creator. In this space, we recognize that there is no such thing as death, only a lifting of the veil that separates the temporal from the eternal.

There is only the ONE Creator and you and I are necessary and essential components of that divine body and mind. It is only through our modern eyes that we judge such rituals of sacrifice as brutal and inhumane, yet our understanding of the human condition has evolved precisely because of the seemingly brutal and cruel sacrifices made by those that came before us. Across cultures individuals have sacrificed their life, their children, animals and their most cherished possessions. Ritual and myth are metaphors intended to expand understanding and transformation. Their themes inform the aspirations of the human potential for self realization. When societies distort myth and religion in search of power, these rituals become a strategic, staged display of power in order to intimidate and control the masses. The strategy of controlling people through rituals of mass-sacrifice seems to be a common practice of many powerful societies throughout history.

Mass displays of sacrifice have been intended to intimidate the masses in order to elicit their compliance and obedience. The Catholic Church, the new spiritual power of the conquered land, utilized the same images of sacrifice with even greater results. Native ancestors were constantly reminded that Jesus had died for their sins. People were intimidated into obedience or simply destroyed when they failed to comply. The conquered generations learned to fear God, to suffer, and to toil in the fields of the new land owners. The conquered people served without expecting relief until death liberated their souls from earth into the cleansing way-station of purgatory and ultimately, for the few deserving, the ascension to heaven. Even at death, no one was assured safety. The length of time spent in a personal, cleansing purgatory was directly correlated to the good deeds performed while living. Being obedient and fearful of eternal damnation kept everyone in line and subservient. God was untouchable and quick to anger. Once again, through the myth of purgatory, the flesh is transformed by fire, molded into pure spirit and prepared for heaven.

We still celebrate this transformation of the flesh today, particularly in Catholic mass. Through the power of the Eucharist, an ordinary piece of bread becomes flesh and blood of the living Christ. When consumed, one takes in the spirit of the Son of God, which now resides within each one. These rituals show us symbolically that we are not separate from our own transformative potential. We are not separated from the Divine. We learn about ourselves from the contributions made by every culture in the world. The Native American Sun Dancers, the Roman games at the Coliseum, even Monday Night Football, are practices and rituals considered violent by many, but all of these examples teach something about the endurance and the capability of the human spirit to eliminate any obstacle or fear on the path to greatness.

Sacrifice is necessary, but not for the Creator's benefit. The ritual of sacrifice is necessary for the one celebrating to connect and to tap into the unseen power of creation and transformation. The ritual of sacrifice allows a physical vehicle to transport, to let go of something you previously held on to, believing it essential, but which in reality was only distracting you from your intention. The promise of transformation is embedded in each story and every example of personal sacrifice.

An example of this great transformation can be directly observed when you consider the sacrifice many parents make in order to secure a better future for their children. Throughout generations, many parents have left their homelands, risking death and humiliation in order to save their children from perpetual misery. So often your parents have made a promise to be better parents to you than their parents were to them.

These stories depict the enduring essence of the human spirit. Always, the spirit knows that there is a promise of something greater on the other side. That promise is the engine that propels us forward. The myths of sacrifice, whether of *Tonatiuh* or of Jesus, are essentially the same. These stories are mythological promises of transcendence inherent to you from your past relations and past generations. These stories serve as a roadmap for growth and a confirmation that one day, when you come to know the truth about yourself, you too will be able to step out of the confusion of your mind and will embrace your higher self.

I Need a Guarantee

Before you take one step in any uncharted direction, you tend to want guarantees that the changes you are about to embark upon will truly enrich your life. Because you allow fear to govern, you live with one foot in the past and one foot in the future, unable to commit fully to your present life. You live in the past because you keep reviewing the mistakes you've made. The suffering you have endured stays fresh and familiar. You have internalized the hurt others inflicted upon you so deeply and personally, that now you don't need the abuser to be around. You are quite capable of remembering and repeating, in great detail, the injuries that were inflicted upon you. The person(s) who hurt you have gone on with their lives and hardly think about you anymore; but you continue to relive the pain and injury, expecting somehow that the world will assume responsibility and correct the injustices you suffered.

You look towards the future as a means of magically bypassing the present moment. You begin to create a future world, much better than your current reality. This future world, you imagine, will bring you riches beyond imagination, fame beyond comprehension, and an indescribable feeling of joy and bliss. Why wouldn't you believe this? You have, after all, been taught that if you work hard enough and play by the rules, there is nothing you cannot achieve. There is no greater myth than the one that promises equality and justice in exchange of blind obedience. Believing that you will be cared for by someone else, you do little to care for yourself.

Sooner or later you will realize that the only force that can liberate and empower you is not a force found outside of you. If you have one foot in the past and one in the future, you are not standing firmly in your present. The present is the only moment that truly matters. The only guarantee that you have is this very moment in which you breathe. Freeing yourself in the present is the only way to increase your standing in the future. Putting to rest your past hurts, torments and sorrows is the only means of getting rid of the extra baggage that holds you back from growth.

The human spirit has always been driven by the instinct to survive, thrive, and to find happiness. You and I have lived and have come to know firsthand, the agony experienced by a young family torn apart by distance and poverty in order to search for a better life. There are countless stories of young mothers who leave their sons and daughters with relatives and acquaintances in order to secure their future food and shelter in lands that are distant and hostile. You know of the young men who leave their new families and the safety of home to labor under the hot sun just to send back enough for others to survive. These stories are as old as time and they take place in any culture where there is a disproportionate distribution of material and economic wealth. The human spirit is in constant search of growth, development and expression. It tends to move towards greater expression without requiring a guarantee of safety or reward. The human spirit moves, compelled by a drive to survive, guided by the compass of faith and its connection to the universal spirit of creation.

When hunger and poverty seem to dominate and it seems that death and despair are the only other options, the human spirit and the instinct to survive are stronger than any fear. Somehow life finds a way to endure. The human spirit is resilient and strong. It has been solidified as a result of thousands of years of transformative experiences. The human spirit learns and adapts to whatever condition imposed upon it. The challenges, barriers, and wars imposed upon us teach us all about the true nature and the power of the force found in every single life.

Even when you are unable to see a guarantee, have faith and know that the universal laws of consciousness always operate to multiply the imprint of your thoughts. Keep your thoughts focused and tuned to the goodness of the universe and goodness will multiply in your life. When you cannot see the next step, hold on and know that nothing can be taken away from you without it being replaced by something greater. What awaits you is greater and better than anything your mind can conceive. The pain and loneliness you may feel today is the preparation required to enter into your new life.

False Safety and False Self

The universal creative force works for good. You may look at your life and feel that you cannot relate to this truth because your existence so far has possibly been comprised of one big loss after another. If it seems you are always giving something away and ending up with nothing, you may be confusing sacrifice for something else. You may believe you are sacrificing when in actuality you are probably holding on tightly out of fear of loss. Conversely, you may think you give out of love, when in reality you give to control. You may fear letting go of anything, believing if you let go you will be left with nothing. You hold on until you see evidence that your efforts will be rewarded.

True sacrifice is directly connected to faith. You cannot give something away with one hand while with the other you are looking for retribution, reward and compensation. Looking outward for recognition of your goodness is only evidence that your false self fears rejection, change and growth. Your false self is insecure and frightened. It attempts to hold on to its limited perception of reality and fears the vastness of the universal potential. Your false self is uncertain and unstable. It fears the power of enlightenment which represents a direct threat to its existence.

Your ancestors believed that by giving away what they were most attached to, namely the illusion of the self as separate from the Creator and community, they were instantly liberated from the bonds of desire and were reconnected to the universal source of all creation. The illusion of death is defeated by the power of faith and the power of the mind. As in the embedded messages of all myths, the significance is found, not so much in the literal translation, as in the metaphoric significance and in the living of the message.

That thing which you call your "self" is one of the greatest sources of false security. You have built your entire existence centered on the notion that your "self" is the only thing worth your time and energy. You have minimized the importance of family and friends in order to defend and solidify this frail concept of your "self". Ironically, the more energy and resources you invest on this vague self, the more isolated you tend to become.

By being overly self focused, you begin to exist as an anxious, fearful and mistrustful individual. You feel a need to constantly look over your shoulder to assure no one is going to attack or take from you. You develop defenses and ready yourself to retaliate and to protect an illusion. You see danger and perceived threat from anyone who remotely looks, acts or thinks differently than you. It is not your fault you think this way. All of your life, you have been on guard, protecting yourself from mistreatment. You have been taught to compete, to focus on yourself and eliminate your competition. You have been taught that this is a dog-eat-dog world and you must get your own.

Life is the greatest teacher and sooner or later you discover you cannot live a life solely focused on personal enrichment and growth if it has no connection to anyone or anything around you. This is a certain recipe for isolation, depression and anxiety. Look around your community and recognize the number of people that live in this fear and dread. When you live only for yourself, your life has a limited capacity to influence anything. Your life takes on meaning and significance only when you recognize that your existence has a reciprocal effect on everyone you meet. By connecting and giving to others, you begin to appreciate your contributions to the greater plan of which you are a vital author and creator. By connecting and giving to others, you begin to see some expression of the Creator reflected in yourself and in everyone else you meet.

False Generosity

There are times when giving and generosity are responses that come, not from the heart, but from the conscious or unconscious desire to control someone else's behavior. This is false generosity. When you are falsely taught that you are undeserving, you learn to give and give, even what you don't have, so that by giving to others they may take notice of your generous nature and give you the love and acceptance you desperately crave. Giving in this fashion does not expand the energy of true gratitude. The energy of true gratitude states that whatsoever you give from the heart will come back to you in a multiplied fashion. The energy of false generosity also multiplies, but in the form of more resentment, frustration and disappointment, not gratitude and not love from others. If you give and expect for others to take notice of your generosity and self sacrifice, you will come to resent the person that is the very focus of your attention. That person will never fully appreciate you the way you expect. The more you give, the more they expect for you to keep giving.

You may, for example, feel yourself generous and giving and yet wonder why people keep taking advantage of you. You may feel that while you are constantly giving, you never seem to get the opportunity to receive. The world may truly feel lopsided and unfair. You give while others simply take. You may truly feel you have no hidden motive in giving. You give because you are a giving person! Maybe you are giving with the hope and expectation that someone will recognize you are worthy of love. Maybe you give hoping for the day when someone you love will turn to you and finally say, "You are really generous and sweet, and I love you for that." You give away that which you most cherish in hopes that you can internalize some of the love and acceptance you feel you lack. You see love and acceptance as external to you. In this case, your giving is not a sacrifice, but an indirect ploy to get someone to love you.

In order for you to receive all that you deserve and all that you desire, you first and foremost must be honest and direct with yourself, even when you may see traits you don't particularly find attractive. When you give, you must give fully from the heart, expecting nothing in return, not even a thank you. The moment you expect something in return, you set yourself up for disappointment. In the simple act of giving, your joy and happiness will instantly multiply. It is because of this natural joy in giving that what you give will be returned to you in multiplied fashion. It is the feeling, the personal sense of reward, which stimulates the duplication of that energy.

There are instances and circumstances which you knowingly or unknowingly orchestrate. There are relationships and situations which you direct and manipulate. These experiences validate your perception of the world, but they can leave you feeling more empty and alone than before. In order to exchange your world for the great paradise of the Fifth Sun, you must be willing to let go of the people that hold you back, the places that scare you, and the limited perspective of fear and lack. You must be willing to let go of certain relationships and connections which do not serve your good.

Another example of false generosity occurs when others do for you, for the purpose of controlling your behavior. So many people will say they are your greatest supporter. They will run to do the least thing for you and expect the greatest amount of indebtedness. Lend low and charge high might be their motto. Personal favors are seen as a form of high credit debt, very much like credit cards and high interest loans which seem to be charged at higher rates to those most desperate. Many people might lend you a hand only if you remember you owe them a favor. They will swear eternal undying love if you only do everything they ask you to do. These are not examples of generosity. These are attempts to control and manipulate others through indebtedness.

If you are hungry for help, affection and inclusion, you are more likely to become influenced by those whose generosity will come at a high cost. A desperate person, hungry for love and approval, cannot distinguish true love from the pretence of love given for purposes of manipulation. There are many actors out there willing to take advantage of the evolving person. Don't be confused. Our ancestors traded a great wealth for a handful of glass mirror pieces. They would later discover that the shiny stone is not always a valuable diamond. While your heart knows nothing else but to give, be aware that not all takers are worthy recipients. Only certain seeds fall in fertile ground. You will never be completely satisfied or safe when you rely heavily on external forces for internal needs. You will never experience true freedom and you will not recognize that true giving is never conditional. True giving never has strings attached. Giving and gratitude are spontaneous, selfless acts that instantly multiply, but only when they are sincere.

Confront Your Fears

Living in today's society, it is difficult to escape being bombarded by strong and persistent fear-based messages that are schizophrenic enough to drive anyone mad. Today, so much of society seems caught up in fear of anything or anyone that is different. News reports broadcast constant threats of terrorism, violence, poverty, racial hatred, economic dominance, manipulation, intolerance and wars all over the world. Today you are not living in the same world as yesterday, where a neighbor could stop by your house and be a welcomed visitor. So often, you have been the target of hatred and resentment and that reality has made you cautious and mistrustful. Recalling past hurts and bottled up pain, you shrink from a world that seems increasingly more hostile. Isolated, you become afraid of everyone and everything, yet you are not supposed to give in or give voice to those fears. To admit to these fears might mean that you have lost personal control and a sense of direction.

So, what are your fears? You must first be willing to recognize and know your fears before you can begin work on eradicating them. Fears are not just those extreme physical reactions when watching a scary movie. Fear is not just your heart beating faster. It is not just the lack of breath, or the sensation of skin crawling. Fears are also represented by those comfortable and familiar things you surround yourself with so as not to experience change.

Once you recognize that you hold fear, you can check with your body to see where this fear is kept. There are times when fear hides in your shoulders as tension. Other times fear hides in your chest as your heart begins to beat faster and anxiety mounts. Recognizing where your fear is stored, you can begin to place a name on the sensation. Let your mind wander and begin to connect your reactions to a specific event, feeling, word or idea associated with that tension and stress. Images and words will begin to surface. These images and words are clues that should be encouraged. You will begin to recognize that, though you may not know the exact nature and extent of your fear, there are signs that point the way. There is nothing wrong with being afraid. What creates a great deal of damage in our lives is having fears to which we don't give a voice. How do you fight against an enemy you don't even know you have?

Most of us grew up knowing fear all too well, but we have largely ignored its presence and impact in our lives. When you see others who appear to be doing well and who appear to have it all under control, you try to fit in and you learn to keep your feelings to yourself, especially your fears. When pain and fear are locked away, they begin to fester, creating and occupying greater space in your mind. You may feel that by creating barriers and walls, your fears and problems are safely locked away. This technique might work well for a while, but it doesn't work forever. At some point, you begin to distance yourself so much from pain, fear and emotional agony that you stop knowing exactly what is wrong. You slowly begin to feel as though life has lost its flavor. You might have a vague notion that something is missing, but your need to suppress your true feelings causes you to misread or ignore clues that can connect you to your genuine experience.

Feelings and emotions can reveal the intimate experience of reality, but certain false myths teach that allowing others to see inside the experience of the soul represents vulnerability and weakness. These teachings were adaptive once. Our ancestors had to be strong and stoic. Any demonstration of weakness resulted in severe punishment, but these old ways of coping with feelings and emotions still linger. Men are still taught to be strong and not demonstrate any sign of weakness since people might consider you less than masculine. Women might be allowed to cry, but they are likely to be harshly judged as weak and "emotional" and are quietly punished for demonstration of affect. You were not encouraged to speak about your feelings and emotions. When you experienced emotional pain and sadness, you had to hide your tears. If someone saw you crying, you would be accused of being a sissy or being highly sentimental. These messages made you fear your emotions and your vulnerability. As a result, you close off your feelings to the point where you no longer recognize when you are experiencing any emotion that might be considered negative or painful.

What you don't confront takes on a greater and greater significance in your life. The blind spots forged by pain and fear create a rigid mold in your thoughts and soon all that you can see and perceive are tainted by the pain of your past. You cannot confront what you fear because you impulsively retract from anything that causes you pain. You lose the ability to adequately label your experiences. You may have some vague feeling that you are not feeling well, but you cannot explain what is happening to you. Without being able to understand or explain what is happening, there is little you are able to do to change the emotions that have now taken control of your behavior. Your emotions control you and not the other way around. You adopt a tough exterior to prove to the world that you have it all under control, yet behind closed doors you might feel fragile or numb. This tough exterior takes a great deal of work to maintain. It hardens your sensitivity and your ability to distinguish the varying degrees of emotions and it keeps people away from you so that you feel safe. By isolating yourself from others and from your own feelings, you reinforce your tendency to be violent towards yourself and you dwarf your emotional intelligence.

Fear can be a great instructor or it can be the greatest detriment to growth. As a child, being afraid of falling kept you from stepping too close to the edge. As you grew, you learned to venture beyond your comfort level and you were rewarded as you learned that the world was much broader than you had previously thought. You could take risks because you felt safe and protected by your parents and those that cared about you. If you have never experienced safety, the entire world represents danger and everyone is suspect.

The language of emotions works like any other type of language. When you learn to speak, the words that you formulate have a close relationship with the object or experience you are trying to communicate. The word "chair" for example, becomes significant because you learn to associate it with the piece of furniture designed for sitting. As time passes and you have a broader experience with more chairs, you become confident labeling all kinds of chairs. Even though one may look very different than another, you learn to generalize.

Emotions work the same way as naming chairs. When you were a baby, your mother comforted you when you were not feeling well. When you lost or broke your favorite toy, your mother might have said, "That's alright honey, don't be sad. Mommy will take care of it." You then learned that when you lose something you valued, you called that empty feeling "sadness". But if your mother was not around or you were punished for showing emotion, you are going to lack the appropriate language and the appropriate "feeling" to associate the word with the felt sense of sadness. If you are never allowed to express your emotions, you have no reference point for words that describe the way you feel. You may be like many people who only know when they have a general sense that something is not right. They may say they are feeling bad or bored, but do not know that their emotions are really much more complicated than just feeling "bad".

Julian, a 40-year-old professional Mexican-American man stated that he has been taking medication for many years to "level off" his "moodiness". He stated that he usually feels very elated on weekends, but the start of the week is always such a downer. Julian believes he is bipolar. This is the Western label and myth that he has adopted to explain his reality. Julian struggles to survive between a world of corporate achievement and economic success, while he also does his best to hold on to his family and culture. Always, behind his thoughts, is a nagging sense that he has not achieved the level of success he'd imagined. Julian stands between two opposing worlds, the world of success and the fear of failure. He divides his life between the world of family and business, joy and despair. Pulled by different loyalties and aware of his own anchoring, Julian is no longer certain of his footing. He adopts a label for his experiences which fits a majority perspective, but which does not take into consideration the complexity of his cultural and individual journey. Julian blames himself for not being good enough. This is the only explanation he has for his unhappiness. On the weekends, he drinks to relax and enjoy himself. The first part of the week, he is depressed, partly as a side effect from the alcohol and partly the results of his returning to work and a routine he does not enjoy and cannot endorse any longer.

Julian is "bipolar" because he believes himself to be so. He is also a person with a strong ancestral background trying to force his experience into a majority perspective. What Julian cannot see is that his unhappiness is trying to communicate something to him. Julian's *tonalli*, his intention and divine purpose, keeps pressing forward, insisting that Julian have the courage to embrace the life within. Julian is not happy at work because work does not satisfy his unique intention. Once Julian becomes receptive to the *tonalli* within him, he will be guided towards his happiness. He must confront his fear of failure and must let go of whatever limiting concept of success he still entertains.

When you don't understand the reasons and motivations for your emotional responses, your mind will create situations and opportunities designed to illustrate your lack of awareness. All of this effort is orchestrated for your personal growth. People and circumstances will appear which will seem similar to what you have experienced in the past. If you are not open to considering the similarities of your experiences, you can feel stuck in an endless repetitive pattern. Taking an interest in discovering the language of your own emotions and validating your feelings will liberate you from having to repeat circumstances that are harmful to you. When you understand the source of your feelings, you will no longer need to punish yourself or keep yourself away from happiness. You will come to understand that every experience is put in motion simply to teach the way to happiness, fulfillment and joy. If you resist the message, the lesson must endure. If you resist the lesson, you will find yourself in familiar situations with different actors

105

unfolding the same drama on different stages. Stop the repetitive cycle by decoding the pattern of unhealthy behaviors. The truth is always simple, elegant and liberating.

You cannot talk yourself into happiness and fulfillment if you secretly doubt you deserve goodness. You cannot step into your present life with joy if your past is pulling you back. Label these feelings and thoughts. Learn to decode the secret language they hold. The reason why these past painful thoughts are still with you is because you have given them great importance, although perhaps unknowingly. Some held pain or resentment is not allowing you to move forward. Your pain is demanding recognition. Recognize and label the experience and make a conscious decision to forgive and let go.

The unknown and unidentified factors within the source of your pain will always keep you looking back. You cannot welcome goodness and embrace the universal creative power if:

1. You believe bad things always happen to you and
2. You cannot reasonably explain why bad things happened to you.

You judge the world based on your current limited understanding and perception. When you are in pain, your focus relates to all the pain you are capable of experiencing. You are certain that what happened to you is bad, maybe even evil, therefore God must not exist or HE would not allow your suffering. Our Creator, or the universe or the power of your mind, whatever you call the creative force, creates certain opportunities so that you might be transformed from the ordinary to the extraordinary. You would not know the transformative power of forgiveness if you never had anything or anyone to forgive.

No doubt you must have experienced great pain and suffered greatly in the past, but in experiencing such depths of suffering, you have also learned the power of your resilience and sensitivity. You've come to know the power you have for forgiveness and for transformation. The force that guides you is stronger than any past circumstance and stronger than any personality that might be intent on limiting your growth. You have come this far for a reason. While such reason may not be readily apparent to you, know that your growth and development have been gently guided by the protective love of the ancestors and the Creator.

If you have the courage to face your hidden fears, you will discover the teaching purpose fear has served in your life. Recognize the lesson and you will grow and move forward to the next stage of your transformation. Aren't you glad there have been fears and disappointments in your life? Don't you feel you have been provided plenty of material to work with for your transmutation?

Lesson: Locate the Source of Your Fear

It is important to define your fears in words that have personal significance to you. Create a comfortable and secure place for yourself. Sit quietly, breathe in deeply and exhale through your mouth. Allow your fears to come and visit you. You may choose to close your eyes. See your fear in your mind and trace it back to its point of origin. See the details around you as you would have seen them in that first original time. Be aware of your body's reaction. Does your heart begin to beat faster? Do your hands get clammy? Are you tensing your shoulders or back? Let the fear come gently. If you feel yourself overwhelmed, take a deep breath. Go as far as you can before you stop and then come back to the exercise at another time. Close your eyes and imagine going down into a basement with

107

many boxes. Imagine that inside these boxes are fears you've stored away. Some of these boxes are very large, others medium to small. The biggest box contains your biggest fear. Approach the box of your choice slowly until you are able to look inside and see your fear. Evaluate your tension and stress. As you begin to visualize and experience your fears, assess your level of discomfort. Close the box and leave it in the imaginary basement until next time.

Take note of your reaction and repeat the experience by visualizing your fear in greater detail. You will notice that with repetition, the intensity of your fear diminishes. Being aware of how you carry tension and fear can begin to break the connection between the past and your present response. Write down as much of your story as you can trace back and label the source of the fears. What is it that keeps you back? If you can understand the reasons why you've held on to old pain this long, then you can learn to forgive, heal and let go. You no longer need to suffer the past. It is like passing GO on the MONOPOLY board game and collecting your two hundred dollars on the way through! You begin to play life at a different level when you can decode the secret messages of your hidden fears. As you reclaim control of your own mind, you will find there is nothing to hold you back.

Forgive Yourself

Sometimes, the hardest challenge before us is being able to believe in our goodness and learn to forgive ourselves for the burdens of the past. Maria is a sixty-year-old mother of six. She came to the U.S. from Mexico in the early seventies. Not long after meeting her, Maria related the story of how painful it had been for her to leave her native home, leaving behind four of her children to be cared for by sisters and relatives. Although it was only two years before Maria had her entire family reunited, the scars that remained left a permanent mark on her psychological make-up.

Thirty years later, Maria has not been able to forgive herself for leaving her children behind.

Maria is not just plagued by her past decision. She is also tormented by memories of her own childhood experience of abandonment. Maria's mother was busy raising many children and so Maria was raised by her grandmother. Although she enjoyed living with her grandmother, she felt rejected by her own mother. Thirty years ago, Maria and her husband were young parents attempting to raise a family in severe economic hardship. She and her husband felt there was no other solution but to flee the surrounding threat of starvation and search for a better life. In so doing, Maria found herself leaving her children behind, thus repeating patterns of behavior she swore she would never repeat.

The unexamined past has a great hold on our evolving life. Maria was likely to repeat past patterns because she was unaware just how deeply these issues of abandonment are embedded in her self concept. After so many years and after each one of her children has become a successful, independent adult, Maria still constantly revisits her decision, simultaneously punishing herself and attempting to convince herself that leaving her young children for two years in Mexico was her only choice. There is not one day that she doesn't ask herself what else she could have done. If her boys have any problems coping with their lives, she blames herself, thinking their troubles today stem from her abandonment then. Is she right? Is she wrong? Clearly, Maria still holds herself accountable and culpable for something that, back then, she felt was the best response to a threatening situation. If she is not able to forgive herself and move forward, there is no one else that can release her from that sense of guilt and culpability, not even her own sons.

Regardless of what you have done in the past, you must forgive yourself and tell yourself that you did the very best you could under the circumstances. Every one of your apparent mistakes was colored by your interpretation, your psychological resources and your perceived ability to defend yourself from threats. Your personal sense of mastery over the world has a great deal to do with the amount of trust and validation you received in the past, particularly from your parents who were charged with your care and welfare. If you grew up in a home that was safe and consistent, you are more likely to be confident and capable of exploring the world around you. If your childhood home was rocked by violence, lack, inconsistency and chaos, then you are more likely to be tentative and fearful.

Perhaps you heard false messages from those that blamed you for their shortcomings. Remember that you are not to blame for anyone else's suffering. Those that might blame you are incapable of taking personal responsibility for their actions. Perhaps you were blamed for your parents' unhappiness and their personal frustrations. These messages, when repeated early and frequently, become permanently engrained in your mind. They are played over and over like a broken record, coloring your experience and understanding. You may be a mature and self sufficient adult, yet the messages from long ago continue to make their way into your present life. You tend not to examine the validity of these false imbedded messages because, over the years, you've lost the objective ability to question your perceptions. You don't wonder if these false messages are right or wrong because they are automatic thoughts that seem to have been there forever. Rather than question these statements, you organize your conceptualization of reality around them. You judge the present, based on your perceived faults from the past.

You and I know many people like Maria who felt their best chance of survival was to leave relationships, children and loved ones behind. Yet, so many years later, these same individuals continue to agonize over their decision, blaming and wondering if they could have, should have done something different. These same individuals are still overpowered, consumed and dominated by an old sense of guilt, self criticism and sadness that does not allow for growth and forward movement. Letting go of pain and suffering and embracing joy is a constant, daily decision that requires commitment and discipline.

Are you still blaming and punishing yourself for things that happened to you long ago? Are you stuck in guilt and self punitive behaviors because others have not forgiven you? What do you need to see, hear or experience before you are able to forgive yourself? Recognize that you are a child of the Fifth Sun, perfect and complete. There is nothing that you have ever done, nothing that was done to you or said to you, which can change that. The tendency to blame yourself comes from the limited understanding of a child's mind who feels injured and responsible. There is no reason to continue carrying guilt and responsibility for matters from your past. The past, no matter how harmful it was, holds no power over you. You deserve to be rid of all the past injuries. To continue to punish yourself does not, in any way, help your current circumstances. Stop blaming yourself. Learn to forgive and become truly liberated from the past.

Feeling Stuck

Sometimes, when it seems pain and suffering is unbearable, you tell yourself you want things to change, but often change is exactly what you fear most. Change takes place constantly; but under stress and pain, you often want to limit change in order to feel in control of a seemingly chaotic reality. When you open yourself up to change, you will feel a great deal of resistance and opposition from this fragile concept of the "self".

This opposition to change comes from the comfort and security provided by doing things the same old familiar way. You develop a sense of self because you hold on to memories and images that constantly change, but which collectively, give you a perception of permanence and sense of continuation. Every moment is lived uniquely and separately and nothing is permanent, not even a mountain. Change is difficult to integrate and accept because you tend to feel out of control. Yet, as you step up and embrace change, despite the fear and uncertainty you may experience, you will move forward. Sooner or later you recognize that the experience of stepping up and stepping forward in faith has enriched your life and you have not really lost anything in the process, other than your past fears and limitations. Catch yourself taking risks, celebrate yourself and you will be rewarded handsomely.

Often, when it seems that you have lost all that you ever had and all that you ever loved, that is usually the moment before greatness is manifested. In moments of darkness hold on and know that something great is about to take place. Your life is shifting. The pain and discomfort are evidences of that fact, so don't hold on to it. Keep it light and positive. Welcome the changes and do not be afraid; what you may currently perceive as a loss, you will come to recognize as a blessing.

In order to rise above, you must believe that your mind has the ability to transcend whatever limitations you have willingly or unwillingly placed upon it. You must sacrifice your routine and comfort in order to confront your demons head on, knowing fully that once you stand up and stare into the face of your darkness, you will inevitably find there is nothing but shadows that disappear in the light. Your ancestors, the *curanderos* of old, used to induce a spiritual vision in which the "patient" was visited by the spirit of their fears. Prior to inducing a vision quest, the patient was given a stick infused with healing powers. Under the healing vision spell, when fears became real, the patient threw the magic stick at the materialized fears and these fears disappeared. You will come to know that darkness is nothing other than the absence of light. Shine the light of truth on your fears and watch them disappear into nothingness.

6

Cultivating the Ancient Path while Moving Towards the Future Self

You can alter your life so that you are living every moment in the best possible of worlds. By aligning your life to live according to the ancestral path, you liberate your *tonalli*, your intention and full potential. Learn to alter damaging thoughts in order to be in line with the creative universal force. Learn to change thoughts which no longer serve you and heal those thoughts of limitation, pain and damage. Changing these thoughts will require commitment, discipline and constant practice.

Cultivate the ancient path by learning to attend fully to your present. Detach yourself from your impulsive and immediate reactions in order to see a world that is timeless and eternal. When you practice this timeless and eternal path, you will inevitably stimulate into action a rewarding, prosperous and purposeful life. This is the path inherent to us by our elders. The intuitive knowledge that comes from a deep reflection on the lessons of the past serves as a map that marks the way of life of a world ever present and available in our collective consciousness. This path has been synonymous of a way of life lived with respect, balance and harmony with nature. This path includes the scientific, spiritual and practical legacy of our ancestors who were fierce searchers of truth and whose lives were a total commitment to these universal principles.

At the center of our ancestors' view of existence is an importance in maintaining a life of harmony, collaboration and unity with community and with every element. The teachings of the past represent a code of principles still relevant and readily applicable in our present lives. Our ancestors lived life governed by their belief in core concepts such as *love, faith, hope, respect, compassion and humility.* They lived these principles with a mindful celebration of life that included rituals and practices intended to bring harmony, health and balance. If you learn to develop a discipline that includes daily meditation, self awareness, mindfulness and active thought reconstruction, you will be able to distance yourself from the harmful components of the false self you have internalized. Once you become aware of negative thoughts and behaviors, you can set out to change them. Practice your path with fixed consistency and you will find your life enriched.

Love

The first principle and unifying force of all life is love. Love is the creative force behind every thing. Although love is an invisible force, you know that it exists. Love is the power and the law that the universe uses to create and recreate itself. Some have said love is synonymous with God. Love cannot choose to be or not and when love attempts to hold and possess, it ceases to be love and becomes simply another object to collect. Love as possession is merely an expression of insecurity, inferiority and fear of separation.

In this consumer society, we all tend to see love as a fixed commodity, something to be possessed, controlled and traded. You tend to feel broken hearted whenever the object of your love does not do what you want and you feel a strong sense of rejection. You feel you lack control and want to defend against the felt rejection by retaliating against either yourself or the person who is the object of your affections. You fall in love with someone and are very enthralled with that person; but whenever the superficial attraction fades, you try desperately to change the person into someone else, someone who closer fits your fantasy of what you believe love ought to be. If your love would only be more romantic, or more affectionate, or more sexual, then you would be truly happy.

When the object of your love is not able to change in the manner you wish, you dump them for someone else, someone who will love you the way you desire. You find another person to love and the immediate attraction carries you for a while. Once the novelty fades, you find yourself focused on that person's faults, and once again, demand that they change.

In this fashion, you can experience the disappointment and heart break that comes from one failed relationship after another. You may feel miserable, but instead of committing to changing your life, you blame the other person for your misery and you get yourself off the hook, at least for now. Your expectation of what a relationship ought to be often gets in the way of what your relationship can be. What can be is always a much greater, broader, more abundant version of life than compared to the version created by your limited understanding of what you "think" life ought to be.

There are no clearer examples of the tendency to blame and control love than the examples offered through many Mexican songs. Old Mexican songs allow us to feel and express pain at a level of freedom we would not be comfortable expressing publicly. Personal suffering is viewed as being caused by an object out of our control. Particularly for men, the inability to take personal responsibility for one's emotions is projected on to the object of our love who did not behave in the manner that we expected. Consider the song *"Tu-Solo Tu" (You- only You).*

The singer laments:

"Mira como ando mujer por tu querer; Borracho y apasionado nomas por tu amor."

(Look at how I've been, woman, because of your love. Drunk and full of passion only for your love.)

In case there is any doubt of who is to blame, the singer declares:

"Tu! Solo tu! Eres causa de todo mi llanto de mi desencanto y desesperacion."

(You! Only you! Are the cause of all of my crying, my disenchantment and desperation)

We can almost see an obsessed and love sick Jose Alfredo Jimenez crying into his drink when he experienced rejection from his queen. Consider his song "Ella":

"Me canse de rogarle. Me canse de desirle que llo sin ella de pena muero. Ya no quiso escucharme. Si sus labios se abrieron fue pa desirme, 'Ya no te Quiero'. Yo senti que mi vida, se perdia en un abismo, profundo y negro como mi suerte. Quise ayar el olvido, al estilo Jalisco, pero aquellos mariachis y aquel tequila me hizieron llorar."

(I got tired of begging her. I got tired of telling her that without her I would die of sorrow. She no longer wanted to hear me. If her lips ever parted, it was to tell me, 'I no longer love you!' I felt that my life was being lost in an abyss, profound and black, just like my fortune.

I wanted to find oblivion, Jalisco style! But those mariachis and that Tequila made me cry!)

Despite his clear rejection and even in the midst of his most vulnerable state, Jose shows that he remains in control of the situation. He clarifies that she wanted to stay after all, but destiny had already decided his fate.

More than songs from our past, these *rancheras* are scripts that shape our behavior and attitudes about our concept of ourselves, of love and relationships. Love becomes a power struggle, a means of manipulating, coercing and controlling the object of our desires. Like a child who does not get what he wants, we throw a temper tantrum to draw attention to the pain of our broken heart. This point is well illustrated in the classic song "Sombras" or "Shadows", made popular by Javier Solis.

"Quisiera abrir lentamente mis venas. Mi sangre toda perderla a tus pies, para poderte demostrar que amar no puedo mas, y entonces-morir después. Y sin embargo tus ojos azules, azul que llevan el cielo y el mar, viven serrados para mí, sin ver que estoy aquí, perdido en mi soledad. Sombras nada mas, acariciando mis manos. Sombras nada más, en el temblor de mi voz. Pude ser feliz, y estoy en vida muriendo y entre lágrimas viviendo este drama sin final. "

(I wish I could open my veins slowly; all of my blood to spill at your feet. That way, I would be able to show you that I can't love any deeper, and then I would die. And yet, despite it all, your blue eyes, the same blue as the seas and the heavens, still close themselves to me without being able to see that I am lost in my loneliness. These are shadows only, which caress my hands. These are shadows only found in the shaking of my voice. I could have been happy, but instead I am dying by living this endless drama.)

We have been conditioned to see love as something happening outside of ourselves. We blame others for our misery and perceived lack when we feel pain and loss. But love is an inside job. Love radiates from inside out and not the other way around. The object of your love and affection is like a mirror, projecting an image of yourself. If you are not content with what you see, don't blame anyone else. Look within and ask yourself how you are contributing to the situation at hand. When you criticize and attack your partner, when you belittle and insult, you are actually seeing parts of yourself that you do not like.

Since it is much easier for you to see other people's short comings, you tend to see in others those unattractive aspects of yourself and you attack externally what you are not able to address internally. If you do not like the person you are inside, you will tend to see everyone as inadequate and insufficient. You must have love for yourself as a requirement to experience true love for someone else. You cannot give away something you do not have. You must feel that there is something inside of yourself worth loving in order to attract others to you. You cannot feel self love if you have never experienced or don't believe you have experienced love at all.

As a child, you may have wondered if you were ever loved because so much was happening around you. Your parents were likely very young, almost children themselves, trying to raise a family in hopes of a better tomorrow. They might have grown up in a home where basic survival depended on strength and emotional stoicism. Love and affection are essential nutrients for basic development. Children want love and affection more than anything else in the world. Physical touch IS nourishment that feeds the very soul. In this world of fear and competition, we've come to minimize the importance of human touch and contact. Without the ability to connect physically to another, we become like robots, logical, calculated, removed and unable to feel true depth or empathy for another.

Young people often confuse the need for love with physical and sexual desire precisely because they are starving for connection and approval. This is one reason why young children who are neglected are in particular danger of sexual abuse. Children become targets for those who see their vulnerability and know they can be controlled and manipulated with inappropriate touch. Children starving for affection become uncertain of themselves and of their surrounding world; and therefore, as adults they often lack the foundation necessary to build boundaries and healthy relationships with others.

So many people are lacking the necessary foundation of self love required to generate love for others. If you perceive yourself to be lacking in self love, you will approach any relationship as a negotiation of affection, a business transaction of sorts and not a true giving of love. If you are starving for love, you will feel yourself needing to purchase love. You might make yourself overly available, giving too much, doing too much, in order to coerce the other into loving you. You will appear to be overly generous and overly tolerant, but it is all a farce. You turn yourself into a doormat, allowing yourself to be stepped on in order to have love stay. You become fearful that if you assert yourself, if you stand up for what you truly feel and believe, the object of your love might leave you. You have attracted someone into your life that knows your vulnerabilities and stays with you precisely because you do not care enough about yourself to defend your own interests.

What you have is an arrangement, not a loving relationship. The object of your love stays because it is a good arrangement that ends when the fantasy falls apart. You have agreed to give up or give away your own voice and needs, in order for love to stay. What you give away is your connection to your truth! That truth is the voice inside of you which tells you that you deserve all the love in the world simply for being who you are. As you fear getting rid of relationships that are not genuine and you hesitate to act in your best interest, your internal voice may quiet down, but it never fully fades away.

There is nothing you have to do to get someone to love you. There is nothing you CAN do to get someone to love you. If you look inside and feel only emptiness, it is no wonder you would try to retain the object of your desires at any cost. The person you see as your love becomes your lifeline. You feel you must possess them because you will perish without them. What you are reacting to is the emptiness you feel inside, which only is covered over when someone else shows you affection. You feel the other is the source of love, but the true and only source of love is inside you, full and complete, just waiting for you to discover your own healing and restorative power.

While it is essential to be loved simply for who you are, it is just as important to know you cannot change anyone. You may fall in love with someone who may not be who you want, but you stay because you feel you could change them someday. No matter how hard you may try and no matter how much you may think that changing the other is for their benefit, you will be miserable and unsuccessful if you insist they change. If you are in a relationship believing that some day he or she will change, you better recognize that you are living in a fantasy. Don't project your relationship into the future, believing that whatever you don't have right now you will have later. If you don't have whatever you desire in your relationship right now, chances are you will not get it tomorrow either. Take a good look at what you have and either love the person just as they are or move on.

It is never too late to embark upon the search of self love. More than a search, this is really a reunion and reconnection to a force and power that has always waited for your recognition and awareness. No matter how damaging your past has been, no matter what harm was done to you, the source of self love remains intact and accessible to you the moment you choose to embark upon the required journey of self discovery. Discovering love of yourself is one of the most illuminating experiences of life. Self discovery is not the end point of the journey, but it is the purpose of the journey and the journey itself. The pursuit of self love is indeed the purpose of our human existence. Self love can also be one of the most painful experiences encountered, as you shed past assumptions and let go of old notions of what you thought your life would look like. There is always pain in letting go of the familiar, even when the familiar is causing you great harm. Don't wait around another day hoping for someone to give you what you believe is missing in your life. Tell yourself that from today on, you will no longer hold anyone else responsible for your happiness.

Faith and Hope

In every myth of every culture across the span of history, faith in an invisible power of creation has been a central concept guiding human development, civilization and growth. Although hard science teaches that reality is what is observable, measurable, quantifiable and able to be duplicated, there are universal forces that are not completely understood by our limited human consciousness.

Having faith in the universal and invisible creative power allows you to transcend the limited trappings of your human form. Faith means trusting that you don't have to carry the burden and responsibility for everything that happens. What a relief to know that you are supported every step of the way, that all is well and that you only need to clear away worry and doubt in order for faith to flourish. Faith fuels our dreams and aspirations, weaving today and yesterday into a timeless tapestry more complex and more perfect than what can be perceived with the physical senses. This is why it is important to keep moving and hoping, even when everything seems to be telling you the contrary.

What you are able to perceive is limited. What you believe to be real is often only a trick of your senses. This is why it is important to not judge what you think is real. What you consider to be real is only a possibility in an endless sequence of potential possibilities. Quantum physics teaches that reality comes into focus only after you, the observer, fixes your attention on what you observe. You are living a world of endless possibilities. Where and what you focus your attention upon becomes your reality. The moment of your choosing defines both your reality and your eternity. You are choosing and creating your life every second of your existence. You are orchestrating your eternal universe with every moment of your conscious awareness. You have the power to change everything in your life. Do you have the courage to give up the comforts of what has been thus far for the excitement of your awakening potential?

Without faith in knowing that you are intended for something greater, you can live life in a fixed routine without any desire or passion to fuel your path. You can give in to the constant demands and criticisms of a society that uses you as a token in a complex, consumer driven existence. Without faith in your connection to something greater, without hope for a tomorrow where your experiences matter, you can become numb to life and exist without living. There is a divinely unique purpose for your life. The second you step out in faith, you will be assisted by invisible hands. The right people, the right contacts, the right situations will make themselves known to you if you remain open. All you need to do is be willing to take that first step and move in the direction of your higher self.

Compassion

Compassion asks that you give up your individual cross and share yourself with the rest of the world and recognize that you are not alone.

Often, pity passes for compassion. Compassion can look at someone's suffering and support that individual's journey without judgment and without an impulse to rescue. Compassion is a higher value than pity, which is feeling sorry for a person. Feeling sorry for someone else's pain puts you in the seat of the judge. No one can truly know the life journey of another soul. While you can easily feel sorry for yourself or for someone else, compassion requires you to let go of your individual suffering and the smallness of your world in order to care more deeply for someone else.

Our ancestors lived with an intimate connection to every individual in their community. They depended on everyone else for their survival. In a world of fear, it is easy to doubt that we have a connection to anything or anyone else. We feel alone and lost in an individually centered society where every person is looking out for themselves and everyone else is represented as merely competition to be eliminated.

You and I grew up hearing our mothers, grandmothers calling us *pobresitos (poor little ones)*. That term of endearment sounds sweet and innocent but it also serves as a constant reminder of our perceived impoverished, helpless and hopeless condition. It is easy to understand why our grandparents, beaten and defeated by generations of servitude and poverty, might have given up on the hope of changing the here and now. They set

125

their sights on the rewards of an afterlife as a means of coping with the suffering endured on earth. They wore their identity as "pobres" with pride and honor.

The classic Pedro Infante film, "Nosotros Los Pobres" (We the Poor, 1946), quickly became the most popular, biggest box office film Mexico has ever seen. The movie became synonymous with the poor, the oppressed, and the Mexican experience. "Nosotros Los Pobres" became the decisive moment in film that articulated our popular culture with the collective experience of the twentieth century. The film depicts Pepe and his family fighting an endless battle of melodramatic injustices. "Nosotros Los Pobres" became part of our collective experience precisely because it spoke to so many of the "pobresitos" everywhere. Ismael Rodriguez, the film's director, stated that he "never imagined how this film would conquer the hearts of poor craftsmen, small merchants, field workers who'd just arrived to the big city, leaving their small parcel of land behind."

In a world that revolves around catering to the temperamental needs of the self, it is easy to lose the capacity to feel compassion. The more you cater to this false "self" the more you see yourself as separate from everyone else. We are living in a society governed by information and competition. Happiness has come to be defined according to the possessions and power an individual is able to accumulate. You distance yourself from your past and your pain because such a past reminds you of your perceived inferiority, particularly as you compare yourself to the rich and powerful. You might deny your higher self and you might re-invent yourself as a hyper achiever in order to survive in the world of competition. In the back of your mind there is that fear that your inadequacies might show through and demolish the structure and tentative hold you have accumulated. You might feel as though you are "passing" or pretending to be hyper competent in order to keep others and yourself from focusing on the shortcomings.

Feeling excluded and separated from the political powers that determine every day life, you tend to withdraw into a life of passive acceptance and apathy. Compassion seems dead and you no longer feel any connection to anyone, much less feel you can impact the world that surrounds you. This sense of helplessness has been imbedded in our collective experience. The "pobresito" has become our modern myth and individual script for martyrdom. It is this modern collective myth which places the burden of proof and responsibility on corrupt political systems, on racism and other forms of mistreatment that attempt to distort the ability to soar. No doubt inequality, racism and other forms of oppression exist, but you must be able to maintain your focus on the ability of your mind to transcend the most oppressive of circumstances. By holding firm to your dreams and intentions, you will overcome any barrier imposed by personalities, by conditions, by the past and present circumstances. Despite the messages of martyrdom and suffering which are so often reinforced by politics and religion, remember that you are not a *pobresito*.

Distancing ourselves from our individual pain in no way minimizes the truth of our past pain. Yet, the past must remain in the past. You cannot keep referencing your identity and you cannot claim your true potential based on your past misery. You can become so overly identified with your pain that you are unable and unwilling to recognize your ability and capacity to transcend the past. There is something intensely perverse about identifying with pain and allowing yourself to be carried into the depths of suffering. Your perception of yourself becomes synonymous with feeling intense levels of suffering; soon, unless you are experiencing intense pain, you are not able to feel alive. You begin to look externally for release from these intense experiences, and in that fashion, you solicit pity and concern from others, often without even being aware of doing so. Other times, you might seek comfort in the mystical shortcuts, like drugs and alcohol. These short cuts might offer an instant escape, but such escape is always temporary and elusive. Hungry for connection and compassion, you find yourself alone and imagine that your suffering is like no one else's.

Compassion describes the highest peak of our human experience precisely because we are able to rise above and beyond our perception of ourselves. Compassion allows the self to die on the high altar of the holiest temple and gives the self over to the greater benefit of the collective good. Through compassion you are able to divorce yourself from your individual experience of pain and suffering. Without being able to do this, you are sucked into a deep well of self indulged pain. Your world shrinks to exclude everyone else and you soon recognize that you care about no one else and in turn that no one else cares about you.

Compassion is also shared suffering. It requires a valiant venturing into the uncharted lands beyond the experience of "self", beyond the borders and territories that divide "us" from "them". When you allow yourself to feel compassion, you experience a deep desire and want to alleviate and reduce the suffering of those around you. In the process, you forget about your own problems and as you are not paying attention to what is wrong in your life, your problems seem to shrink and disappear. Compassion goes beyond your individual experience and individual emotional suffering. You are able to forget about your own drama and become much more concerned with wanting to alleviate the suffering of others. You begin to see the strength of the connection you share with others regardless of apparent differences. You are able to see how others, just like you, wish to be free of pain and suffering. You see how, because of their emotions and their individual circumstances, others are unable to find that freedom. Your struggles and your experiences become synonymous with the experiences of the other. You wish freedom from suffering for everyone precisely because you are able to relate and see yourself intimately connected to this web of life.

You might hold on to your sorrow and pain like a badge. Your pain can become like an old war wound which keeps you from moving beyond the scars. Maintaining the *pobresito* mentality only attracts more pain and more suffering. You may temporarily attract others to your life, for example, because they feel pity and sorrow for you. Sooner or later you learn that those relationships are based, not on compassion, but on a power differential. These relationships depend on you feeling inferior, damaged and scarred. If you play out your script of a *pobresito*, you are going to attract someone who needs to rescue you. That person relies on their need to control. This relationship cannot grow beyond these limitations. No matter how intense your experience of past pain might have been, the important thing to remember is that you survived. THAT is what speaks to your strength and resilience. What protective power has carried you forth and guided you to this point? Why have you endured as much as you have if not because of some divine purpose? Ask yourself how the lessons you have acquired through these years have contributed in making you the wonderful and resourceful human being you are today?

Respect:

Another central discipline inherent to us is the concept of *respeto* (respect). Cultivating self respect and respect for others is an essential ingredient in creating a peaceful and harmonious coexistence. Respect recognizes the intrinsic worth of life and as such, it is a value that grows as it is reflected back.

Respect cannot be purchased, traded, bought or sold, but must be earned. Respect is reciprocal. In order to earn someone's respect you have to give it first. Regardless of the perceived or actual status of the other person, respect must be a two way street. Respect is the attitude of acknowledgment for the feelings of the other. It is the esteem you have for the sense of worth of another person. You respect someone because there is something about that person that makes their value clear to you. You recognize in the other the same divine spark you recognize in yourself. You feel that sense of respect in great part because you are also able to see yourself reflected and valued in that person's experience. Due to the respect that you have for another, you do not interfere with their rights and their autonomy. You seek to help and not harm because you are able to appreciate your connection and relationship.

So often RESPECT has been imposed, demanded by those in power and authority. The demands for respect automatically imply not only a power differential but a presumed superiority on the part of the one who makes the demand. This is not respect, but intimidation. You have been taught to respect those who have more power, education, money or status than you. As a child, you might have come to believe that respect meant doing without questioning. You might have thought that respect meant you had to allow yourself to be directed and corrected by others who were supposed to be superior somehow.

It is disrespectful, for example, to have a school system that discounts your experience and does not allow you to see yourself reflected in the lessons you are taught. You watch your parents being mistreated at work and in society. You want to be included and be a part of the larger society, so you begin to distance yourself from your parents because you have internalized the message that somehow they are inferior and do not deserve your respect. There is an intense rage that begins to build inside and soon you think that the only way to get respect is to demand it by force.

This is one of the reasons why we are losing so many children to gangs. Gangs understand the old concepts of respect, honor, family and loyalty to a past. They understand these concepts as marketing and recruitment tools. Gangs are also entrenched and confused about power, wealth and might as they duplicate the same dominant system and structure of power which oppresses them. Gangs become blinded by their own hunger for power and money and soon the corrupt leadership is easily manipulated and removed. We must work hard to save our children by reclaiming and re-teaching the power of the undistorted and uncorrupted past.

When you feel disrespected and mistreated by others, when you feel that your experiences and opinions are discounted as irrelevant, you might grow tired of the fight. You might begin to develop automatic beliefs that such mistreatments are valid and you might begin to disrespect yourself. Everybody who mistreats you and disrespects you must be right and you must be wrong! Soon, disrespecting yourself happens with greater frequency and with greater intensity.

You have internalized and personalized so many negative criticisms and devaluations of your person that it is easy to lose sight of your self love and your sense of self respect. When you lack this sense of self respect, you end up getting in the way of what is best for you. You find countless ways of ruining situations that could yield your happiness. You break up relationships because the person is not who you thought they were. You walk away from jobs because you feel insulted and disrespected. You harbor feelings of unworthiness and therefore are constantly projecting outwardly what you are unable to see inwardly. Indirectly you are attracting people and situations that will leave you feeling further disrespected.

As you feel disrespected, you become hypersensitive to pain. Your hypersensitivity magnifies even potential experiences of disrespect. Sometimes you are able to read these experiences accurately, but most of the time it is your hypersensitivity that influences your misperceptions. Feeling badly, you adopt a devil-may-care attitude and you may seek experiences which confirm your worst beliefs. These experiences cause you to feel guilty and remorseful after offering only a brief escape. You become more likely to hurt yourself because you find some temporary escape that allows you to feel defiant.

Carlos is a child survivor of repeated sexual abuse by different male relatives. As he became an adult, Carlos was confused about his sexual orientation. He says that he has always felt incredibly lonely and separated from everyone. To cope with his loneliness, Carlos engaged in frequent one night sexual encounters with other men. Carlos feels guilty, damaged and rejected. He desperately looks for someone to love him and to find that someone, Carlos goes from one encounter to the next. Inevitably, the one night stands never develop into any significant relationship. Each time, Carlos ends up feeling hurt, lonely and used. He tries to fill that sense of emptiness by going out and engaging in another one night stand, always looking to fill the emptiness he feels inside.

Without a mutual give and take, respect can become confused with an oppressive means of getting others to be subservient. You cannot make anyone respect you out of fear. You cannot yell at children to behave, insulting their intelligence, and then demand that they respect you. Having children be afraid of you is not the same thing as earning their respect. Although you may view your children as not having the same rights as you do, your children can only learn respect from you when you learn to acknowledge their humanity and their respective rights for self expression.

Children have a right to feel safe, to feel love and affection, to feel they can expect their individuality and their uniqueness to be celebrated. When children have these basic necessities met, they will be better able to give you the respect you demand. When you grow up being disrespected, you learn to disrespect yourself and others. You may learn that your experiences and personal reactions do not matter. If others mistreat you and disrespect your rights, why would you be concerned about the rights of others? Disrespected and mistreated, you begin to internalize your own oppression.

When you experience constant disrespect of your rights, you might retaliate with anger and resentment. When you act in defiance against individuals or groups that attempt to deny your happiness, you are likely going to be judged as a rebel, antisocial, or even a criminal. You might transfer that same disrespect you receive and come to resent authority figures who insist on denying your equality. Your experience of reality is discounted while you seek to assert yourself, yelling out the injustice of it all, while nobody seems to listen. Your voice and your message become louder and you find yourself alone, beaten down, shouting against the wind and fighting against the tide. This popular myth that highlights the superiority of some over the inferiority of others discounts your true nature. It is a distortion even while it may seem to be shared by all of society. You soon believe that you are wrong in defending your true worth.

Humility

If you want the world to treat you as someone who matters, you first have to believe in your own self worth. Many of us have been taught to be humble, but too often we have come to interpret humility as meaning we have to put ourselves below everyone else. The ancestors taught that humility was turning yourself into nothing so that you could become one with everything. The ancestral teachings of humility included emptying of the self, not as a means of degrading or diminishing oneself, quite the contrary. By practicing the suspension of self, you are able to experience true union with all creation.

As a child, you were likely taught to humble yourself in front of everyone because everyone else had more worth than you. Teachers, priests, doctors, lawyers, everyone else besides you, had the right to ask and demand anything and it was your duty to comply. This lesson of humility is not taught to everyone equally. There are many children who grew up hearing they are the most important person in the world. Developmental psychology teaches that infants pass through a stage of development called "healthy narcissism" in which they have their every need anticipated by an attentive and loving mother. This stage of development is considered necessary for the development of the self as capable and valuable. Imagine how differently children develop if instead of teaching them that they are the most important person, we teach them that everyone else in the world matters more than they do. Humility then, is not the idea that you should feel or act inferior to anyone else around you. Humility is the sense that, as great and wonderful as you might be, you still only know and comprehend the tip of the iceberg of your potential. Humility is the recognition that there is a power much greater than yourself operating in and through your existence and that, in moments of despair, pride and arrogance, allowing this power to guide your life, means surrendering to the idea that you are truly a child of the Divine on a journey back home.

Eliminating False Safety

There are times when you might experience life as one constant threat after another. In response to those external threats, you can become addicted to the perceived sense of safety and you can confuse safety for rigidity. The person who never leaves their home becomes a prisoner of their false sense of safety. A child who is never allowed to explore becomes fearful and insecure. When your world seems chaotic and frantic, playing it safe can provide a false sense of security. The perception of safety can become just another coveted possession. You tend to hoard those things which you lacked and the sense of safety is no different. Rigid routines can give you the false notion that you are in control of your environment. You can decide to stay right where you are even though your current situation might make you miserable. You comfort yourself by saying that at least you can predict what will happen next.

If you say you want love in your life, but spend much of your time bemoaning and obsessing about the love you did not receive in the past, you will only attract individuals who will eventually prove your worst fears. This is because you are looking at life through your pain and sense of lack. There are many people who are walking around believing there is no love in the world, yet they hunger for connection and for the love they say is not available. They play it safe. They do not get involved with anyone too deeply and their lack of involvement is used as evidence for why the world has no love. You cannot, for example, simultaneously believe there is no love in the world and tell yourself you are looking for love. Sometimes, when we feel we are playing life safely, we are merely asking the universe to support two contradictory desires which end up canceling each other out. If you feel that you did not experience love, affection and approval in your past, you may strongly believe and desire love in your present life. Despite this very real and strong desire for affection, the thoughts of lack are more powerful and they can cause you to miss evidence of love. Because you are not at peace with your past, the past must make its way into your present life to help you discover what is unresolved and thus keeping you from moving forward.

Resilience

Have you ever accomplished something which you were certain was impossible? By accomplishing what you thought was out of reach, you learn to push the limits of your potential. You go beyond your own imagination. What you previously thought impossible becomes another benchmark that you've obtained because you have been able to push yourself beyond your own self imposed limitations. You grow stronger with each challenge and soon you are certain that there is nothing you cannot accomplish.

Despite more than five hundred years of a confused and altered history, much of the original spirit and many of the collective wishes of your ancestors still endure. While Mexico, along with much of Latin America, has been through an endless string of rebellions, revolutions and upheavals, the spirit of survival of its children remains stronger than ever. Despite tragic losses of culture, tradition, myth and history, the experience of the children of the Fifth Sun endures, because ours is a story of survival. The burning away and the experience of loss were necessary to prepare for the moment of self realization.

Many times it seems as though some undefined force pulled you from hopeless despair and propelled you forward to the next day. You've come to have faith in this invisible power, this unseen source of strength which presses you forward towards the fulfillment of a greater tomorrow. When you are able to keep your eyes and mind focused on the promise of your Creator, you are able to pull on an invisible and inexhaustible fountain of strength and fortitude. When you allow yourself to be carried away by the anxieties, desperation and depression created by outward appearances and seemingly hopeless situations, you sink into your own reality and begin to lose sight of the invisible hands that are there to hold you up and pull you forward.

There is an embedded compulsion to repeat the same struggles, the same challenges that your parents and grandparents had to confront. The burden and responsibility of past lives can weigh heavily upon your shoulders, particularly if you are not aware of the significance of your ancestors' contribution to your personal story. Without a sense of what has happened before you, past myths and conflicts still find their expression in your individual life, but you might not be able to see the patterns. By knowing your past, you can benefit from the victories of your ancestors and learn from the greatest of their mistakes. The price of these lessons has already been paid for you. The path before you is clear and unobstructed if you only believe and learn from those to whom you are connected. Tap into your past connections and you tap into the very essence and source of your resilience. Tap into the potential of your present life which is made possible by the contributions of the past. The past lives of your ancestors have created a roadmap, a trail to be followed that is lit with the very stars which illuminate the path to your destiny.

There is no doubt that you are resilient. You can tolerate great pain and suffering, but there is no need to obsess about the scars and hold on to pain as a means of identification. Along this journey, there are no extra points for constant suffering and for living a life of martyrdom.

You are a resilient being with a strong central core. You are a child of a long line of warriors, sages and healers who have encountered great oppressive forces and obstacles and yet their lessons and gifts still survive. Despite the many challenges your ancestors encountered, they drew upon that sense of resiliency to secure the survival of a new generation, your generation!

Lesson: Pain Passes

There may be times when you feel your personal journey has been filled with much pain, anguish and rejection. You may be tired and feel you cannot go on another day, but know that it is only the external appearance of events which is drawing your attention. It is your own judgment, based on limited information, which is causing you to draw such conclusions. In times of despair and anguish, it is most important that you learn to go within. Learn to listen to your inner voice and hold on to the light within which is the source of your strength. Precisely because you are resilient, it is important to practice self care. What do you do to care for yourself? We often wait for someone else to care for us the way only we can care for ourselves.

You cannot go from one crisis to another without beginning to react to the stress that results from a life of chaos and loss. Stress and reactions to stress can become part of your very personality. So often, that feeling of tension and that sense of fight or flight can become as addictive as any drug. There are many people who have not known what a healthy or normal life is. Chaos and confusion, uncertainty and conflict are all they've ever known. Breathe and know that however bad the current experience may seem, it is indeed transitory and it will inevitably give way to some other experience that is better. Think of the many obstacles you have been able to overcome already. Think of the challenges your ancestors had to overcome and know that all that strength is available within you right now.

Fear, vulnerability, increased violence and greed can leave you feeling uncertain as to when your personal situation can improve. It is difficult to have faith in a world that is abundant and loving when you are constantly focusing on the things you don't have. This heightened stress and unhappiness can cause you to fall victim to a permanent state of burnout and exhaustion. You endure and survive somehow, but seldom do you check to see the collective damage caused by prolonged exposure to crises. You begin to feel that self care and self nurturance are luxuries you cannot afford. You often neglect your ability for self care because you are too busy preparing for the next emergency. It is time to stop that circular motion and step back to appreciate the larger patterns of your life. Remember that you possess a built-in power to heal any circumstance including any current pain, illness and suffering.

Lesson: Remain Calm

As you begin to label and know your fears by their proper names, you will begin to address them and speak to them directly. As you speak your fears, they will automatically become threatened. Simply speaking their identity and their name challenges their existence. You may become confused and anxious over the overwhelming evidence of change beginning to happen around you and this feels frightening, new and threatening. For many civilizations, the bull has been a symbol of the power and force of our fears. Bullfighters replicate the dance of courage and victory of reason over fear. The bullfighter celebrates an ancient ritual by facing his charging demons and fears in the form of a raging bull using nothing but the strength of character and a red cape. The challenge is to remain calm amidst the perceived danger. If you turn around and run in fear, you will inevitably find that your abrupt actions will surely increase the anger of the bull. Although it seems contrary to our natural impulse to run away, the best way to attack a frightening thought or painful memory is simply not to run in the opposite direction, but to firmly and calmly hold your ground.

Lesson: Take One Step

One of the most important themes in the substance abuse and recovery community reminds us to take life ONE STEP AT A TIME. This simple statement serves as a reminder that we must not allow our anxiety and tensions to get the best of us.

Be kind to yourself. Don't berate and insult yourself for having allowed things to have gotten out of hand. Take some time and create a list of all of the things you feel need to be accomplished in order for you to feel that you are back in charge of your life. Break down your list into parts to be completed within a realistic and manageable time frame. If you find that your initial list is still too optimistic, be willing to revise your time frame. Above all, be mindful to not allow harsh criticism to come into your mind. Confront any negative judgments about your perceived lack of progress. When you reach and accomplish a benchmark on your list, give yourself praise and recognition for having reached this point.

7

Yourself and Others

Who you are is a reflection of the values, ideals and aspirations of the group or individuals you most admire and who have influenced your development the most. Developing in an optimum environment means that you grow amongst a community that supports and shapes every aspect of your life. Your surrounding community gives you the encouragement and support you might need in challenging moments. Community members and extended family are there to guide and protect you. Yet, many of us have not grown up in an optimum environment.

Our culture and community of origin has often been devastated by forces of oppression, poverty and inequality. The notion of community implies common beliefs, customs and practices, but when a group feels that such beliefs and customs are under attack, the group begins to separate from those values which define their hopes and aspirations. When a community adopts the historical and mythical legends that attempt to re-label its identity as a minority, a burden and a nuisance, members of that community are likely to internalize these labels. The community loses its strength, union and identity and the individual member absorbs the insecurities of the group and the fears of the majority. Maintaining a connection to the ancestral values is a source of strength, a fortification and confirmation of our identity and a vehicle to transport us into a greater tomorrow. The challenge presented to the children of the Fifth Sun is to maintain such awareness and connection in an environment that is ever changing.

How can you maintain an open heart and an open mind when everything around you seems to change daily? How do you stay focused on loving and growing when you recognize that the world as you have known it must change forever? How do you relate to others when you find yourself growing and changing in ways that leave you feeling different than everyone else? How do you reach beyond your silence, discomfort and personal pain to assure others have access to you and you to them? If you see yourself as a victim, as being powerless and inferior, you will tend to see others as hostile and aggressive.

The ancestral path teaches the importance of maintaining an awareness of the moment as it unfolds, preserving the ancestral teachings and aspirations, unlearning damaging lessons from the past and learning to replace negative and self defeating thoughts. Thoughts are things too. Everything you have ever accomplished, everything that has ever been created, began first as a thought. As such, thoughts are born in your mind but they materialize concretely as you project them into your environment.

Let's Start with Our Children

All of us, whether we are parents or not, serve as role models and guides for the younger generation. Even if you don't wish to be a role model for anyone, you don't really have a choice. All of us come from families and families have children who hear stories about every member in the group. Somewhere someone is looking at your life as either an example to follow or one to avoid. Children look towards the adults and based on their observations, they judge what is possible for their own lives. As adults, we create the examples of what children view as possible for themselves. Children who grow up in an environment where many adults are in jail, addicted or lost to depression and suffering, see themselves projected into that future. Even if they tell themselves they don't want to grow up like that, the constant thought of avoidance increases the likelihood of the behavior occurring. How many times have you said, "I don't want to be like my mother or father", and when you step back and observe, you are doing and behaving just like the parent you've criticized.

What you believe is possible in your life affects not just your individual destiny, but the lives of those that come after you. Children watch their parents and they learn and process every sensory experience to which they are exposed. Children practice the behaviors they observe, but they also pay close attention to the attitudes, body language and unspoken thoughts the adults feel are successfully hidden. If your words and actions don't match, your actions always speak louder than your words. Children are then forced to make sense of their observations and because their minds are still developing, they may draw some interesting conclusions which may never be revealed.

What you do as a parent has a deep and long lasting effect on your child's sense of him or herself and on their ability to feel competent, happy and secure. This is most true and most relevant during those first seven years of life called the formative years. Teaching children the value of the ancestral path and connecting them to a culture of origin gives them a solid base for the formation of an identity rooted in strength, pride and endless potential. All of us have a basic need to feel we belong to something greater than ourselves. Ancestral teachings answer those basic questions of who we are, where we come from and why we are here.

A Word to Parents

To provide a child's base for identity, you must be secure in yourself and be clear in your own values and ideas. If you are rooted in your own identity, you will be able to recognize the natural curiosity of a child and respond to their questions with kindness and a willingness to support their need to explore the world. You will be able to address your child's questions and concerns with empathy and understanding. You will recognize the importance of increasing your involvement in your child's life during this critical time of personality formation.

If your children are to maintain a positive attitude about their identity and their culture, you must be involved in their lives while learning to graciously adapt to the constant changes presented to you. While you are maintaining a connection to the ancestral teachings, you must also maintain a sense of connection to all the constant changes happening around you in order to keep yourself and your children rooted. The greatest predictor of a child's academic success, for example, is directly correlated to the level of parental interest and involvement in a child's school and their studies. In other words, the more interest you take in your child's academic or personal life, the more successful your child is likely to become. To be involved in your child's academic life, you must lose the fear and intimidation that keeps so many parents away from school buildings. How do you rate the quality of your participation in your child's life? How do you rate the participation of your parents in your own childhood? How do you think this experience still impacts your life?

While our ancestral teachings are rooted in tradition, our modern culture is not static. You must, therefore, be flexible and adaptable to the changes that occur around you. You must learn to adapt to the influences and the challenges presented by a modern society. You must learn to do all of this while holding firm the foundations set by your ancestors. These foundations become your anchor in that sea of constant change. If instead of adapting and changing, you are feeling threatened and scared, you may tend to become resentful and withdrawn. Often, you tend to become most resentful against those that are closest to you, in part because you come to believe that those who love you will stick around forever.

You can become resentful of others who seem oblivious to your suffering. Soon you find yourself responding to those around you defensively or even aggressively. When you recognize that this is happening to you, stop and look towards yourself. What is the source of your unhappiness? Somewhere, you are carrying a belief that the world is denying you something. If you can be aware of what you feel is lacking in your life, you can create an approach to address this sense of lack. Be aware of yourself and of the choices you are making. Even if you choose not to withdraw and disconnect, you are making choices that will have future consequences for you and your children.

As you inevitably are compared to other parents and are constantly reminded that other parents do things differently, there might be a tendency to feel insecure about your parenting abilities. Don't allow yourself to be taken over by feelings of inadequacy. Under the pressures of such insecurities you might be tempted to withdraw from your parenting roles and responsibilities. Some parents allow their children, who might have more contact with the majority culture, to dictate the rules. This is never a good idea. Soon, you might experience the role of parent and child beginning to shift. Your children might begin to take on more responsibility and authority than they should, while you withdraw further into isolation and depression.

If you are neglecting your parental responsibilities, know that someone will step in to fill the void. The boundaries between who is the parent and who is the child can often become blurred during this time of uncertainty. This is particularly the case when children are allowed to take on adult responsibilities such as serving as language interpreters or child care workers. I recall such responsibilities from my own childhood with mixed emotions. As an eldest son, I learned the value of hard work, but I also felt socially awkward for many years, thinking most children my age were immature. It took some hard lessons and serious losses for me to appreciate the true value of friendships, spontaneity, fun and love.

Teach your children the values of the past. The dreams of the ancestors have much to teach today. Modern stressors can cause anyone to wonder about their identity. Don't allow your role as a parent to be diminished. These times of change and transition are precisely the times when children need you to be certain of your parental role and authority. Children may gripe and complain about strict parents, but children also desire and hunger for parents who are clear about their limits and their boundaries. Children need to feel someone they trust is in charge. Especially for young people, structure makes the world a much more manageable and less frightening, less intimidating place in which to live.

Stay focused on the universal principles inherent to you by the ancestors. Keep your core grounded in truth and tradition, but don't allow yourself to become rigid and afraid of the changing world of shadows. You must constantly work to stretch yourself and learn by adapting to whatever life deals you. Stretch what you have considered to be your comfort zone.

As you come home from long hours of work, all you might want to do is relax and sit back. Your time at home, particularly if you have children, must be more important than your time at work. Your children need you to be involved in their lives. It does not matter what level of education you might have or how good your English skills might be. If you take the time to speak to your children's teachers and become familiar with the work that is assigned to them, your children will begin to improve their performance in the classroom. Don't allow intimidation about having to speak to the school teachers get the best of you. It is important to fight past these fears and learn about your children's progress and development. Stretch your level of comfort and attend. Take action. Ask questions about your children's academic and behavioral performance in school and sit down on a regular basis with your children to read and to help them with their homework.

If you don't feel you can help, sit and ask questions about what they are doing and have them teach you. Do not allow yourself to fade into the background like another piece of furniture. Fight for your family and for your place within your family. You are worth more than the wallpaper in your house and your children deserve parents who are more than bodies occupying the same living space. What you do for your children you also do for yourself. What you don't do for your children will impact the rest of their lives and yours.

Romantic Relationships

The most fertile ground for self transformation is the realm of passion and romance. We don't die on altars any more, but we still are willing to give our life over for the promise of love. For many, passion has become a dirty word. For children of the Fifth Sun, passion is the flavor of life itself. Today, the meaning of passion has become distorted and confused. Passion means total surrender to pleasure or to pain. Most of the time, we have been re-oriented to identify with passion as intense suffering. We learn to identify with either the passion of the Christ on the cross or the passion of the Aztec brother on the sacrificial altar, both giving of themselves completely to assure the survival of others. Passion however is also the total surrender to the ecstasy of pleasure and the emptiness of eternity which contains all power of creation. Passion can become a curse when it turns into attachment. If you want to possess the object of your desire, you can become the possession of your passion. You desperately attempt to control what is clearly now controlling you.

Relationships work best when you surrender yourself completely to the other, but whenever you become aware of yourself, the sense of separation begins. At this point, you realize the power of your personal need. If the focus of your relationship is to love without asking anything in return, you are likely never to feel unhappy. Often, however, the focus of the relationship is really a focus on the importance of the self. We give to get in return. When the needs of the self outweigh the needs of the other, the relationship suffers. When you love unconditionally, you are less likely to take pain and injury personally. Interestingly enough, the less self focused you are, the more you tend to attract love. What you give always comes back to you in multiplied fashion. Love is never a gamble, for even when love turns out to be a source of pain and sorrow, the lessons embedded in the lived relationships are intended to teach you to love better, fuller and with greater abandonment.

If you are in a relationship where you are being hurt, you must analyze why you stay because such a relationship in not rooted in true love. You don't deserve to be victimized and mistreated by anyone and nobody deserves the weight of your hatred and misery. It is not fair to that person and it is not fair to you. Nobody can be so powerful as to hold you eternally captive and hostage. There is no one in the world that can have power and dominion over your life unless and until you choose to give them such power. Let go of those old myths that say that you must bear the abuse and mistreatment of another. I know many people who have spent decades blaming a partner for their misery and then when the partner gets tired and leaves, they then say they are miserable because their partner left. You have an inherent potential to live a present life full of joy, love, health and abundance.

If you are in a miserable relationship, as much as you may believe your partner may be the worst person ever, you are still in that relationship because you are choosing to stay. There are circumstances in which violence and control become significant parts of a relationship. Even in the most abusive of situations, you must work to understand the nature of your deep rooted thoughts and feelings which contribute to your decision to stay. So many times we participate in situations where we permit mistreatment simply because we have forgotten our true worth. No matter what has happened to you in the past, you don't deserve to be treated poorly. Take charge of your life and take charge for the responsibility of your happiness. Stop spending valuable energy and emotional resources on a relationship you clearly do not believe will grow. When you know that the person you are with is not the person you want to be with, you must find the courage and do them and yourself a favor by acting and letting go.

Do not use the excuse that you will stay with someone who makes you miserable for the sake of the children. Realize that when you are suffering, your children suffer too. Do not sacrifice your life for someone else's happiness, particularly if you believe that your sacrifice somehow makes you a better, more worthwhile person. The period of the human sacrifice has ended. You will come to resent the one you feel made you sacrifice yourself so completely, even, and perhaps especially, when that person is your own son or daughter, husband or wife.

You might get hurt, but keep your heart open anyway. Expressing your emotions might seem contrary to what you have been taught. Your natural reaction might be to hold your feelings close to yourself for fear that someone might exploit your emotions and view you as vulnerable and weak. If you find someone who recognizes you for who you truly are, hold on to them. They will reflect back the great force of love magnified through your connection. Appreciate the gift of such connection and don't squander it by allowing resentments and pettiness to hinder the strength of your bond. Whether you find that bond among people who are your friends, your lovers, your relatives, these relationships define your character and perspective of life.

The unresolved drama of your ancestors' lives still seeks expression through your present embodiment. Frequently hearing family legends gives you a deeper understanding of your parents' motivations and therefore, your own.

Gloria is a seventeen-year-old young woman who was born in Jalisco, Mexico. Gloria's father was a musician and a self described party animal and reformed womanizer. Gloria's family moved into a suburb of Chicago more than two years ago. Gloria has been jealously guarded by her parents, particularly her father, who refuses to allow her to date anyone. He says that he knows what guys are after and will make sure that his daughter never falls for their games. Gloria is dropped off and picked up at school to assure she has no contact with boys. What Gloria's father doesn't know is that she has been secretly seeing Roberto, a young man with a history of expulsions for drug possession.

One day, Gloria stayed out late and was afraid to come home, so she ended up spending the night at her boyfriend's house. The next morning, Gloria realized that she would never be allowed to return home. Today, Gloria's parents don't speak to her. She is pregnant and realizes that her boyfriend has a serious drug addiction. She suffers abuse and mistreatment, but can't ask for help because she feels she deserves everything that is happening to her.

At home, Gloria was protected and guarded so much that she chose the first opportunity to leave home. Whether Gloria is consciously aware of her actions or not, she has internalized a negative view of herself, influenced by the fear and insecurities of an overprotective father. Gloria's father was attempting to protect his daughter from meeting a man like him. Gloria loves her father despite his tendency to control and judge, so it comes as no surprise that Gloria finds someone attractive who shares many of the traits her father once shared. Understand the victories and the challenges of those that came before you and you understand the nature, glory and potential of your own individual life.

Your ancestors were not perfect, but they were humans with an undying commitment to enlightenment and eternal liberation. Their achievements and discoveries are yours to use and apply in your process of transformation. Understand the challenges of your ancestors and you can better understand your own. Armed and protected with this awareness, you are more likely to view others with a deeper sense of respect for their own heritage.

Without a connection to the lessons of the past, you are more likely to view yourself and others with a certain indifference and detachment. Without a sense of connection, you can feel that there is a void that must be filled in order to be happy. Our consumer driven world economy depends on this deep sense of human emptiness and attempts to fill that emptiness with products and images. Be aware of objective images you consume. Notice how these images are portrayed by the television, movies and magazines you read. These images are intended to sell a materialistic way of life that makes people dependent and seeks to control and possess. These images will have you believing that happiness can be found when you have the right car, the right amount of money, the right clothes, the right jewelry, and the right person hanging from your arm.

The ancestors believed that eternity revealed itself in every moment and some aspect of the Creator revealed itself in every person to the one willing to look. This ancestral teaching can be applied to every relationship today, but particularly our romantic relationships. Romantic relationships and partnerships do not happen automatically; they require a constant awareness of the moment, daily re-commitment and maintenance. Ask yourself what you can do to improve the day of the person you care for. What small action or token of your affection can you offer to lighten their load or show that you care?

Don't make the mistake of thinking that because you are married or have someone to share your life with that you no longer have to work at your relationship. In order for any relationship to grow, the spirit of love and the respect for the magic of life must be celebrated continuously. Give thanks that you have someone who loves you and who is willing to share their life with you. Love, after all, is the greatest purpose of life. Your life must feel itself multiplied by the love you are able to give and the love you are open to receive. Discover the divine in yourself and in the other. If you are aware of your divine composition, then you will be able to see the divine reflected in the person you love. Be aware of the awesome experience as it unfolds and be grateful for the feelings that love is able to stir in your heart and soul. Be grateful that you are capable of feeling the depths of compassion and the unselfishness found when you give yourself over without requiring anything in return.

Conformity and Addiction

You can give in to a life lived from a false self and you can tell yourself you are content, but sooner or later, the little voice inside you, the same voice you've been trying to keep quiet, begins to knock at your door, demanding to be heard. The harder you try to ignore your inner voice, the more persistent these messages will become. The nagging feelings and persistent thoughts that you are living incongruently become so loud, and occupy so much of your psychological resources, that you may seek ways of numbing the pain. For many people, alcohol and drug addiction become a chosen vehicle of escape, finding that substances can provide a temporary distraction from a life that has become too painful to manage. With time, drugs and alcohol, instead of making you forget, cause you to relive in greater pain and detail, the troubles of your past. You find that you have to drink more or ingest more drugs to keep yourself from feeling miserable. Yet, you start to feel more miserable than ever because drugs and alcohol are causing your crash.

Becoming addicted to substances can confirm internalized negative messages. Angie, a client of mine, stated that when she informed her father she had a serious drinking problem, her father responded to her, "I am not surprised; I always knew you would end up an alcoholic." How much has Angie been impacted and influenced by her father's thoughts and beliefs?

People who abuse substances are seeking to chemically alter a reality that seems unbearable. Yet the picture of reality is distorted by past injuries and the resulting sense of isolation. Drugs and alcohol take their toll on your body and mind. Without the necessary energy to feel good, drugs and alcohol pull you into a depression and sense of hopelessness from which it is difficult to rise. Drug and alcohol addiction can serve as an escape only for a certain amount of time. Eventually, addiction becomes a greater problem than what you had originally tried to cover.

You stay addicted in large part because you now find yourself in a state of depression caused by the inevitable withdrawals. This pattern of behavior fuels the fear to look at life through sober eyes and a fear of taking personal responsibility for the mishandling of life. The moment that you locate your source of strength, identify the barrier and re-establish your connection to the ancestral teachings, you will be able to attack self damaging thoughts and convert these into self affirming and self supportive thoughts. It is not necessary to adopt superficial or overly optimistic thoughts that dismiss reality. On the contrary, be objective and critical. Test the validity of any thought rationally. Engage in a fact finding dialogue with yourself. Are you truly to blame for everything that has happened to you? Can you really be that bad of a person? Detach yourself from your personal reactions and picture someone just like you telling you their story. What would you tell that person? How judgmental would you become?

In ancestral healing traditions, illness was understood as an imbalance of the self with the natural and universal forces. Because the Creator governs over all of creation, peace and harmony are the natural state of all things, but individuals are free to resist, block or interrupt that perfect peace. If you are feeling ill or unhappy, what must come into re-alignment are your perceptions and your thoughts, not the world. In our ancient past, a person's worth was established, not so much by the individual's life, but by their significance and contributions to the group. Every unique talent and manifestation of behavior was considered a gift of the Creator and so everyone was integrated and useful to the larger group's benefit.

In native culture, individuals became ill whenever they put themselves before the interests of the community and disrupted the delicate balance of all elements. Illness and disease were a community concern because the person suffering was believed to project their imperfection onto others and so the group participated in the reintegration of the individual back to the group. That return to balance consisted of the community surrounding the patient in love and acceptance. The patient was reminded how much they were loved and needed. When one individual became ill, everyone participated in the healing rituals and in the reintegration of the individual back to the family and social structure. Addiction did not exist as a concept. Drugs and mind altering substances were medicinal properties to the ancestors. As such, these substances were consumed mostly during healings, rituals or spiritual ceremonies.

The community healing social structure is familiar to many children of the Fifth Sun. It is still evident in loving extended families that care and look after the well-being of all members. You are familiar with the support that is received from parents, uncles, aunts and everyone who surrounds you with love and assistance whenever the need arises. You know that a family may become angry, bitter, upset or injured somehow, but family always stays together and helps out in times of true need. Yet, as we become more modern and more mainstream, these long held ties to family and communities begin to deteriorate. So many families are dispersed to hostile remote areas, away from connection to the past, to traditions and to loved ones.

In the past, slave families were divided and the members sold. Children and parents were separated, their names and languages were changed and they often never saw each other again. Native families, families of the Fifth Sun, are still being divided and separated by immigration, by poverty and ignorance. This scar in our collective psyche is deep and undeniable. The weight and consequence of this painful past still lingers. Today, many of us still sell ourselves into self imposed oppression in aggressive and violent attempts to defeat all competition and achieve more.

As you become confused by this deep sense of social isolation, you often seek to reconnect by discrediting and distancing yourself from past traditions and customs. You may begin to view any tradition from your culture of origin as inferior and irrelevant. As a child, you may have been taught to forget about your native language and traditions. In your attempts to fit in, you can lose that which makes you unique. Your traditions, your heritage, your very identity can become a source of shame rather than strength and pride.

My parents live in a small town outside the city of Guadalajara. Every time I visit them, I am still struck by the friendly attitude of everyone I meet on the streets. The cows parade through the main streets and the farmer stops to greet the baker. If you are waiting at a bus stop, everyone wishes you a good day. If you are walking down a street, everyone you pass will say good morning or good evening and ask about the neighbors and relatives. Besides being good manners, these greetings immediately connect the individual to the larger group and society. You feel a sense of belonging and a deep affection and compassion for everyone you meet. You recognize everyone as family and you feel yourself a part of that social balance.

Father-Mother God Within

The balance of external elements, of nature and society, is also duplicated within each individual. Your ancestors understood that every living organism represents a balance of opposing forces. All women have elements of the masculine, some to a greater degree than others and likewise with all men. Good exists because of your familiarity with what is bad. The day exists because it is balanced by the night. The Creator is recognized, not as a male figure, but as father/mother God. All forces of creation serve a purpose and are available for your use as you seek to bring into existence the life that you desire.

What the Catholic missionaries attacked most readily was the adoration of the Creator as female. The missionaries enslaved the natives and forced them to destroy the temple to their highest goddess. On top of the ruins of the sacred temple to Mother Creator, the native children were then directed to construct a new cathedral to the new queen of the heavens, the Virgin of Guadalupe. The Virgin of Guadalupe was named after a small Spanish village in the province of Caceres, Spain. The Spaniards believed that Guadalupe sounded very much like the Aztec goddess *Chalchihlicue* (or *Tonantzin*), which, when pronounced correctly, sounds very similar to Guadalupe. By destroying and replacing the temple to the highest goddess, the missionaries also turned the goddess into a virgin and the fourth power in charge of the heavens. The first three powers contain the three in one: the Father, the Son and the Holy Ghost.

For Mexicans, regardless of age, generation or history, the Virgin of Guadalupe is God, is Mother and is Mexico. She represents all of the love, the sacrifice, the caring, the loss, the yearning of a mother wishing for nothing more than to care for her children. No wonder we have brought her image along in struggles for independence and self expression. No wonder she is adored beyond religion and country. There is a love which our Lady of Guadalupe projects that cannot be contained by any human institution, precisely because the Creator as Mother is a powerfully healing myth.

Our Lady of Guadalupe represents the love of our mother, the love of the ancestors, and the love of the transformative experience from one level of awareness to the highest. The transition from ancient Mother God to Guadalupe was never difficult for native children to conceive because they saw their Maternal God looking back at them. Our ancestors taught that God is God, the power of human consciousness, the force of creation and evolution that has no gender, no beginning and no end. God is equal parts male and equal parts female. God is *Mama* and *Tata Dios*. From the remains of mother *Chalchihlicue/Tonantzin* emerges the eternal mother of the heavens, the Guadalupe that always was and always will be.

Lesson: Stay Open to Change

Take good care of yourself. If you feel that there is some past experience of suffering that is blocking you from happiness, identify the source of that pain and begin a systemic process of removing the block. What myths and false teachings have you incorporated that are influencing your pain? Identify the harmful thoughts you still hold and work to let go, forgive and embrace the new awareness. Don't be caught up in fixed patterns of behavior which can make you resistant to change. Keep hold of your dreams, but don't focus so much on the specifics of how this dream should be realized. Let the universe take care of the details. You can perceive changes as traumatic if you focus on specific details and events when these don't match your expectations. You can receive a blessing and not recognize it immediately because you are busy anticipating something else. Trust that the natural rhythm of the universe is orchestrating to bring about all that you desire. Be patient and have faith that the ancestors' plan for your abundant and joyous life must unfold as promised.

Give thanks for all that is good in your life and you increase the likelihood that more good will come your way. Giving thanks is a way of directing the universal, creative force. By giving thanks you say "yes" to the universe and that creative force knows what you desire. Tell someone that you appreciate their presence in your life, that you cherish the time you spend together and watch how your relationship becomes stronger. Identify negative myths and lessons of the past and create a concrete, consistent plan to remove these damaging thoughts from your beliefs. Once you learn to label positive experiences in your life, pause and compliment yourself for the progress made. You will begin to increase your ability to recognize these positive experiences with greater frequency.

8

The Vehicle of Transformation

The greatest healing and transformative power in the world is found right within your very own mind! Yet, to access this power, you must have an appreciation for your own ability to transcend your perceived limitations and shortcomings. Your thoughts are the key to your happiness, wellness and prosperity and your mind is the vehicle that can take you there. Your mind contains the unexplored frontier of endless possibilities. It is the stage that has been set for the greatest and most exciting of all human experiences, the expansion of consciousness, which is the next leap of evolution. Where does this potential for optimal growth and development come from? Where does the power that puts a thought in your mind come from? Where is the power that fuels your muscles and directs the growth of your cells?

There is an awesome mystery capable of interacting with your mind to create a reality that satisfies your deepest desires. This power moves around you and it lives through you. This is the mystery of love and connection of which you are an active participant and a co-creator. Your ancestors felt this mystery and orchestrated every aspect of their daily lives in order to give constant recognition and thanks by ritualizing every action and activity. The ancestors dedicated their lives to the study and revelation of the creative force. In every relationship and through every interaction the ancestors honored this mysterious bond. We all share this universal force and the eternal source of energy and creation.

The universal force of creation is not a person or any specific representation, but it is capable of being expressed in endless forms and manifestations. This universal energy is constant and eternal, regardless of what people choose to call it. Some people have chosen to call it God; others the Creator, *Yahweh*, *Tonantzin*, *Allah* and messengers have always come to every culture, from *Buddha* to *Mohammad* to *Jesus*; all of these prophets describe the same source of love, energy and transformation. The name we use and the discipline we practice to develop a closer connection to this source is irrelevant. What is important is the recognition that you are a necessary part of the total equation and for that reason you are intricately connected to that creative source and to everything and everyone around you. No history and no re-creation or oppression of cultural myths can change that fact.

When you recognize your connection to something greater than your own individual life, you can have the power to penetrate through your sense of isolation and separation. Knowledge of this interconnection gives you access to an unbound source of strength and vitality. This is the connection to the engine that fuels and maintains your mind and maintains perfect equilibrium of your body. It is the same intelligence that also maintains the universe in equal harmony. That power holds a blueprint of the lives your ancestors have lived and that same blueprint is contained in its entirety within your own mind. For centuries, the ancestors discovered that when the stars and planets aligned just right, a portal opened that allowed the transportation of the physical world into the eternal realm. The pyramids and temples in Tenochtitlan were built to replicate the celestial harmony. The ancestors also understood that because you are a microcosm of the universe, when you are in harmony and internal alignment, the energy flows through you and you can directly access the full power of transformation. You can now tap into the ancestral legacy to remove any barrier to happiness and uncover the full potential of your life.

For the ancestors, the power of awareness and consciousness was a gift from a greater power than themselves and yet of themselves. The elders called this power the Creator, but today we might call it the power of human consciousness. This is the ability each of us possesses to connect directly to the source of all creation and the ability to use that source to co-create life as we dare imagine possible. Within your mind are all your individual experiences, the ones that you remember and the ones that you have long forgotten. Within your mind are also all of the collective experiences, wishes and aspirations of the ancestors and of the entire human race. The Creator places all possibilities at your disposal. The ability to rise from oppression and sadness is contained in your mind. The spirit of the one mind and the grand Creator is everything and everywhere at once. The elders had such a deep connection to the evolution of the earth itself that the spirit of creation spoke through the wind, the trees, the animals and the mountains.

The myths of your native culture reveal the rituals and practices the ancestors used to guide and move the force of creation for their benefit. The Creator communed directly with the old relatives, emperors and all other living creatures in order to weave the everyday magical life of everyday people. Elements transform into something greater. The smell of fresh cooked corn transformed by the mesquite woods awakened the senses of the earth. The power of these smells and the power of all collective experiences of the past, still resides in your mind as collective memories. Even if you never remember smelling that smell, when it hits your nose, you instantly know it as the familiar smell of the giving earth which sings joyfully celebrating the ability to feed and nurture life for yet another day. You react to smells, sounds, tastes, textures with the collective mind that holds the experiences of your ancestors.

Because you are made of the same stuff as the earth, the heavens and the universe, you have access to the source of that same power. Your ancestors adored their Creator in all its varied manifestations. People, therefore, adored these various forms as separate deities. At the same time, our ancestors understood that all derived strength and power comes from the ONE and eternal force. Just as you are a separate individual, you are still intricately connected to every other living creature on earth. This is the mystery of the one and the many. Our ancestors believed in a certain universal power that demonstrated itself in and through all creation, yet could never be adequately understood through any one manifestation or expression of itself.

The greatest disease you can acquire is in believing that you are separate from this creative experience. Separation comes when you believe yourself to be either better or worse than everyone else on this planet. In our present society, we are ironically more informed and physically closer together, yet we are further apart from each other than ever before. The more crowded and advanced we become, the more isolated and frightened we tend to feel.

One Pattern: One Source

There is an intelligent pattern occurring in and through every living organism. This pattern is the embedded intelligence which tells a tree the right time to drop its leaves and the right time to bear fruit. This intelligence keeps the planets in orbit and it also tells birds and whales when to migrate. This same intelligence keeps your heart beating, your muscles growing and your brain functioning adequately so that you can breathe, think and feel. This is the nature of the ONE mind. Your individual mind is connected to the universal mind which regulates all life and movement.

The mind is not the same thing as the brain. We can take a brain apart and locate the area where emotions are processed and where senses are interpreted, but we cannot even begin to explain how this process happens. That is the mystery of the mind. This is the mystery that our ancestors have been trying to understand since we first were able to use the gift of reason. Our ancestors looked to the heavens and to all of creation for the source of that power and wisdom. Knowing then that the mind transcends the physical boundaries and our limited understanding of its functions, the ancestors utilized the concept of Creator as an attempt to express the awesome power and eternal force that is beyond comprehension.

The ability of the mind to create, imagine and transform thought into matter is the dwelling place of the Creator. Some of us understand this invisible power more through the language of religion, others through philosophy and others through science; but what is expressed, what is being communicated, is the same truth across all disciplines. Regardless of what field, discipline, or body of knowledge you choose to study, you will discover that the essence of all knowledge always points to the same conclusions, the same truth and to the same mysteries.

Today, more than ever, we are advancing our understanding of the human capacity for healing, for growth and for self actualization. We are expanding upon our current traditional fields of knowledge, including medicine, and we are integrating a more comprehensive view of wellness that embraces a unified approach to mind, body and spiritual healing.

Just as we are expanding the manner in which traditional medicine views health and wellness, we must also broaden the lens through which traditional psychology examines culture, spirituality and human behavior. Psychology is a science based on the observation of human behavior, usually in its abnormal and pathological state. Just as medicine is a science based on the observations of the malfunctions of the body, psychology has been employed to show how far one person can deviate from the pre- approved norms. Psychology typically defines what is wrong with a particular individual who is in pain and looks at human behavior from the perspective of what is not working properly.

We have already learned that whatever you focus your attention upon tends to grow and magnify. Looking at human behavior from a deficit model tends to increase the very deficit being observed. We must constantly insist and encourage the field of psychology to consider the language, culture and reality of so many people who have not been included or considered in the development of theories and treatment approaches. A good psychologist should be like a language translator, using the language of metaphors, myths, world views, history and understanding of the individual's place within the universe in order to effectively communicate the power of healing. A good psychologist becomes a healer by providing true assistance and guidance for the client to be able to find his/her own pathway.

Ultimately however, it is your own faith that will cure you of any ill. The secret energy of any healing is the faith the ill person places in the agent employed to deliver the message of balance and harmony. The entire universe would re-arrange itself to your will if you believed strongly enough that such

THE VEHICLE OF TRANSFORMATION

action was necessary. The changes you desire in your life will be made when you embrace your ability to restructure your thoughts and perceptions. Perhaps you believe in Western medicine but have other complimentary perspectives and understandings of illness and wellness. *Curanderismo* (the native practice of healing) in our Latino cultures for example, stems from our ancestral understanding of healing herbs, song, ritual dance, prayer, *sobadas* (or massages) and other practices designed to stimulate healing. Rather than feel you are ignorant or inferior for having these believes, you should honor your convictions and practice whatever connection you might have to your greater source. It is your faith in this connection which will ultimately bring you everything you need, desire and deserve.

We have always sought to understand the unseen through different lenses. The awesome speed and brute force of the cheetah, the abundance, celestial harmony and mathematical precision of heavenly constellations and the effortless soaring of an eagle are reminders of our eternal union with the power behind it all. Whatever lens you use to contemplate the unseen mystery, it is this lens through which you explain and understand your cosmology, which ultimately defines your life. Assuring your connection to the great mystery of life has been the greatest legacy your ancestors have fought to protect and deliver to you. Know that within the silence of your mind you possess the power to connect directly to a higher source of reasoning and vision. This knowledge will provide you with everything you need. Learn to tap into these quiet spaces through meditation, prayer, silence, ritual or whatever other practice you might use to find the peace contained at your central core.

How You Lost Your Voice

Everyone begins life on this planet possessing all that is needed for a successful and joyful journey on earth. Every limb and every finger represents the sum total of an evolution process that is intelligent and self knowing. Your life represents every collective accomplishment of humanity, including language, culture, religion, science and art. Everything you are, you owe to those ancestors that have contributed their evolutional share in bringing you to this place and time.

When you were an infant, you already possessed the ability to speak any language in the world. In your newborn utterings and mutterings, you duplicated every sound ever made-the building blocks of any and every language on earth. As a newborn, you had the capacity to absorb information at such an astounding rate that your brain was able to double the amount of information processed every couple of months. As a perfect child, you began to encounter the realities of an imperfect world. Hopefully you had the experience of being parented by a mother and father who surrounded you with love and acceptance. When you cried for hunger, you were fed; when you were cold, you were given warmth; when you were frightened you were reassured. Your needs stimulated a response from your parents that resulted in your needs being served. This is how you learned to trust the world around you. Your first teachers were your parents. As a child you wanted nothing more than to please your mom and dad. When you were a child, your parents seemed to be all powerful and all knowing.

By knowing that your thoughts and cries have power to manifest whatever you needed, you came to know the world as a safe, supportive and predictable place. This is how you learned to have a certain sense of mastery over your environment. Even when your parents were not perfect, you

168

learned to cope with their imperfections because you still had a great sense of a consistent and predictable world. When you are a newborn, for example, your mother is attentive to your every sound and to your every cry. You are fed before you even know you are hungry. Your mother looks at you and tells you how wonderful you are. You are made to feel as though you are the center of her world and this feeling gives you a strong sense of confidence and self mastery. Over time, your mother becomes consumed by the business of the world and she also learns to let you cry sometimes. Able to distinguish an emergency cry from an irritable cry, she responds to you, but not as promptly as she used to.

If your parents are still fairly attentive to your needs, you learn to cope with their inconsistencies and short comings. If your parents are completely unpredictable and unavailable to you because of their own emotional injuries and their own psychological pain, they are unlikely to give you the basic attention and love you deserve. If your parents are confused and battered by a violent and chaotic world, they are likely to instill those painful and erroneous experiences in you. A mother who was mistreated by her own parents may not be able to give her own child the love she herself did not receive.

You take your cues about what is right and wrong, what is good and bad from the praise or punishment your parents gave you growing up. The extent to which your mother and father are available to care and love you is directly correlated to your ability to develop self confidence and self reliance. If, as a child, you received more praise and more encouragement, you will develop into an adult with more self confidence, greater ability and capacity for socialization and greater sense of self worth. As an adult you will have a greater capacity towards hearing and trusting your inner voice and intuition.

If, as a child, you heard that you were always doing something wrong, that you were bad, problematic, if you were discouraged from exploring your environment, you will tend to develop a lack of confidence and a lack of mastery of your surrounding world. You will tend to believe the messages you hear from your parents without questioning the validity of the insults. Your parents, as much as they did their best, were only working with the best they had. Your parents themselves were trying to overcome their own childhood traumas and experiences of lack. They might have experienced harm inflicted upon them by their parents, who were hurt by their parents and so on and so on... Every generation wants nothing more than to love stronger and more purely than the previous generation, but we love based on our own understanding and past experiences. If there are blind spots caused by the pain and suffering of the past, these blind spots are also transferred on to the next generation. That is the process of our human evolution. If your parents were taught that the Creator was punitive, vindictive, resentful and to be feared, they will teach you the same and you will fear that force.

To develop healthy and strong, you must feel that you are wanted and that you are in a safe environment. You must feel that you've gotten a good reception for your arrival on this earth and must believe that the world is a loving place. It is this sense of safety that gives you the confidence to venture out of your comfort zone and explore your environment. You can explore because you are not afraid, but excited about the great possibilities to be discovered in this world of love. In a world divided by greed, the accumulation of power and racial superiority, trust can seem like a rare commodity. Some lessons are purposely taught to confuse and to control, but the intuitive knowing that comes from your soul will always lead you to the ever constant truth. Whatever blind spot or false belief you have incorporated can be unlearned. Identify the false belief or myth, repeat it to yourself and then replace it with an affirmation of the truth.

Christopher Columbus' voyage has been credited for proving that the world was not flat, but the impact of that voyage continues to influence our cognitive development today. The world became much larger and more awesome than anyone could have imagined. Today, the world has gotten figuratively smaller, but we are at the same point, discovering that the universe is not flat, but an endless, interactive field of infinite possibilities. The force of creation is not separate from who you are and that force has always been with you through every experience of ecstasy, pain and anguish. The pain and suffering you have endured are caused by actions and thoughts based on misperceptions of the truth. When you identify the irrational thought or harmful myth and replace it with a strong affirmation of the truth, in time, you will be able to see your life improve.

Beliefs about the nature of the world become solidified in your mind and you create patterns of behavior in order to adapt and validate your view of the world. What you believe to be true is played out and reinforced in every aspect of your life. As you become an adult, your thinking becomes more sophisticated but rigid and intellectualized. You might give great rational explanations detailing why you are right and everyone else is wrong, but at the foundation of your personality, you might still hold the core belief that the world is unsafe. You don't tend to challenge these damaging core beliefs because you see evidence to support your thoughts wherever you turn. What you fail to recognize is that it is you who is projecting your history and held notions out into the world, creating the very thing that you hate and fear. Love has not turned its back on you, but you have protected yourself against the vulnerability of love. The world is like a blank screen and you are the film projector, projecting your own movie on to that screen. If you want to change the movie, look inside the projector, not at the manifestation on the screen.

Whenever something reminds you of your pain, you have the tendency to be pulled right back into a negative and dark world of confusion. Your negative thoughts tend to generate more negative thoughts. When you are upset, you can tend to view every experience as a catastrophe. This is why we must be very careful not to say hurtful things to our children. Verbal insults, especially those coming from parents, have a way of sounding more true to children's ears and these insults create the foundation for later self perceptions. Words can stay, carved deeply in memory. Words and insults can linger for a lifetime. Words can create false concepts of God, life and love upon which a damaging and limiting perspective of life is organized. Anyone who repeatedly insults you can become such a powerful force that you can confuse that person's voice as your very own consciousness and thought. The voice you hear guiding you is no longer your own voice, but the voice of the person who has been insulting you. You might begin to repeat to yourself things you heard as a child. "You are no good." "You are stupid, ugly, fat, and lazy." It is most important to examine those messages you might be telling yourself. When you look at yourself in the mirror, what do you see? What do you say? Whose voice do you hear?

Many of us also learned not to ask questions as children. If your parents grew up feeling rigidly controlled and oppressed, they likely passed these messages on to you. "Stop asking so many questions!" "Do as you are told!" "Because I said so, that's why!" These types of responses kill the naturally curious child nature and the innocent hunger for knowledge. A child's curiosity and sense of competence must always be rewarded. A curious mind becomes interested in the mysteries of the world and seeks to find the answers. Curiosity is a felt sense and a faith in an inherent ability to connect to all answers.

Our parents learned from their own parents. They held on to false teachings of inferiority, because at some point they also heard these false messages from others who spoke in a desire to control and manipulate. Our parents might have never known that the oppressive messages and myths they had learned were really distortions of a truth that would be unknowingly transferred to the next generation. The messages become repeated so often and so early in our development that they are internalized. This means that these insults are permanently recorded in our minds and they play back automatically. Understand that your own parents likely grew up in environments less than ideal and are simply repeating the painful and dysfunctional patterns and lessons inflicted upon them.

Many of our recent native elders were disconnected from the telling of an accurate history and the original myths that speak of a royal heritage. Many of these elders never learned to read or write in the language of the new arrivals. They forgot their own language and some even learned to be ashamed of their past. Schools were not accessible for many of our poor ancestors and the education of poor children was seldom a priority in the ranchos and the vast countryside where everyone had to labor under the sun in order to eat and survive. Many of us have heard stories from the elders that describe long and difficult travel on horseback just to be able to attend school long enough to learn the basics of primary education. Schooling often took away from the important duties of caring for the lands and the family. Because of their duties to care for others, many ancestors remained poor and formally uneducated. They held no political voice and often could not read enough to defend themselves.

The experiences of the elders, their struggles and battles for survival, their experiences of oppression and colonization can still survive in your mind. Many of our ancestors never had the ability to contemplate their emotional well-being because they were frequently more concerned about meeting basic needs. Often, families were necessarily large in number in order to have sufficient labor force to work the fields that sustained a way of life. In that sort of environment there are often so many painful experiences that can be transferred from one generation to the next. Many, who grew up fighting for survival, have neglected their emotional and psychological development in an attempt to meet basic survival needs. It is time to reclaim all that has been neglected.

Whatever reaction you have to the events in your life, know that your feelings and thoughts matter. Recognize that your thoughts are a normal reaction to whatever has taken place around you. Your thoughts hold the key to the expression of your true self and should be acknowledged and given voice. Yet, your thoughts are also based on your past experiences. As such, your thoughts provide one emotionally loaded interpretation of events as these unfold.

Do not assume that because you feel a certain way that it means your feelings are giving you the most accurate and unbiased interpretation of what is transpiring around you. Emotions can carry us away from thinking. Emotions ask for expression often without thought. Giving full power to emotions and feelings can leave you vulnerable and wounded.

You are like a radio antenna receiving and transmitting messages. Be curious and remain open minded to the messages that come to you from the universe, be ever mindful and aware. Maintaining an awareness of the moment will allow you to avoid impulsive reactions and the pull of unexamined emotions. Recognize that everything that happens unfolds according to an intelligence we cannot fully comprehend, but which we know always works for good.

Transformation

In order to prepare yourself for the transformation into the next quantum leap of your development, you have to be willing to track your thoughts with an ever watchful eye. Any thoughts that are contrary to your greater good will block your growth. Be aware of these thoughts, learn to name them, and then you can work on altering them. Secondly, you must be willing to let go entirely of the lesser identity you previously held as your reality. This is not easy, because we all get used to life being a certain way and we become familiar even with situations that are not to our benefit.

You are capable of impacting the very nature of the world. Your thoughts orchestrate and form the solid world. The material world is not as permanent as you have imagined. Solid matter is mostly empty space. Learn to see it as such. The material world is not the center of reality. The material world is simply an embodiment of the thoughts you hold and entertain. Change your thinking and you can alter the physical world around you.

A drowning person will indiscriminately grab at anything nearby and often pull down the very person trying to save them. In the sea of confusion and in the waters of despair, you tend to reach out and grab anything to hold in order to keep yourself from drowning. Grabbing indiscriminately when you are in despair can be counterproductive. Those things which you cling to will redirect your developmental energies towards a path that may not necessarily be the path intended for you, but one which is chosen for you by the insecurities of your "self." Sometimes, when you are in despair, the right person will find you. This person might take pity on your pain and help you get back on track. More often than not when you are in despair, you tend to attract people who are in equal or greater despair than you are. You will tend to cling to these lost souls in part because you want to help and rescue, but in greater part because you also need rescuing. You can also become vulnerable to those who are looking for an opportunity.

When two objects collide, their density and speed will determine the magnitude and impact of the collision. This collision can result in an explosion that will send atoms and molecules flying everywhere. Likewise, you are on a similar trajectory. Unlike objects that operate without a mind, you can see ahead and avoid future collisions if you are aware of what you are seeking. As counter intuitive as it may seem, in moments of despair it is most important to be still, do nothing and recognize what you know. If you continue to grab and struggle, you won't know if the person swimming in the water with you is trying to rescue you or drown you. Know that the light and truth that resides within you is greater and stronger than any external appearance of seemingly random events. Be aware of what and who you attract into your life. Be selective and discern what is in your greater good.

If you allow yourself to become dominated by tension, depression and anxiety, you will have a difficult time listening to your inner voice. If you focus on the noisy distractions of all that happens around you, the chaos becomes your identity. You begin to react to everything and everyone with equal intensity. You can adopt a trial and error approach to life, hoping that by this random method you might eventually find the right answer. You become subject to all those myths and legends you've internalized which may describe part of your behavior, but do not speak to the person you truly are. Your transformation begins as you learn to challenge the validity of these damaging thoughts. What cultural myths have you adopted and incorporated into your personal story? Are you the unlucky lover, the lonely child, the martyr, the quiet sufferer? You play out the prescribed drama and suffering embedded in these personal myths without analyzing whether these stories still hold their original meaning for your life.

Lesson: Learning to Hear the Sound of Your Own Voice

Along the journey of life you may be tossed, battered and bruised particularly if you try to meet other people's expectations of who and what you should be. If you insist on meeting other people's expectations, you will begin to lose the ability to listen to that inner voice, the source of your strength, your creativity and true happiness. You can come to doubt yourself and these thoughts can make you feel inferior, unworthy and incapable. Negative and critical thoughts that become incorporated into your awareness will make you doubt yourself. Other people's opinions and expectations may begin to create layers of confusion and soon there is so much clutter in your mind that you cannot easily access your power. In order to function socially, you might develop a different personality or self -- one you feel is safer and more appropriate for public consumption.

You may tend to put away the real you, tucked away some place safe where no one can get to it. Like a mask that you wear to keep others from seeing your true identity, this mask, called a persona, becomes your public self. The persona becomes the part that you show others. This false self protects your vulnerability, and at the same time, it takes you further away from your true self. You invest increasingly more energy and

THE PROMISE OF THE FIFTH SUN

resources on this persona, until it seems that you have become a complete stranger to your innermost true self.

This false self is filled with our insecurities, our tendency to feel superior to others, our competitive nature, our need to satisfy our physical lusts and hungers, our vindictive nature and on and on. The world seems to reward this emphasis on the ego by stimulating your desire to possess, to hold power, to control and manipulate. Letting go of this identity in order to reconnect with your deeper, truer self can be very difficult and disorganizing. As you begin to embark upon the journey of self retrieval, you will encounter all sorts of resistance and rigidity from that ego part of yourself that refuses to let go. Indeed, as your center of reference changes, you have to find meaning and self definition at a much deeper source than the physical world.

If fear, doubt and a painful past have silenced your unique expression, you can reclaim your voice by releasing the past and unblocking the barriers created. There is a central part of your core which sacredly and faithfully holds your individual voice, no matter how much you might have endured. This is where your true self resides, unburdened and untouched by all the traumatic events of your life, no matter how horrible they might have been. This central part of you endures despite any hardship and it remains pure and unaltered by the problems of life. More importantly, this core part of yourself is accessible in its full potential whenever you choose to reclaim its power. This is a place rich with creativity and possibility. This is the never changing kingdom of enlightenment ruled by the god of illumination, the God of the Fifth Sun.

Lesson: Take Pride and Learn from Your Heritage

Your ancestors were proud people. Life was a seamless combination of ritual, myth and reality. Many of the daily recreational and work activities they performed served as a ritual of gratitude and an acknowledgement of the eternal bond humans had with the Creator. Because the ancestors were persecuted for practicing the ancient ways and because they were made to feel ashamed of their identity, today such sense of shame is still a burden carried by many of their descendents. Pride in who you are and pride in your place of origin should not be traits you have to hide. Your individual voice matters and, when united with the voices of others, it has the power to change an entire society.

Political battles for the loyalties and the allegiances of the masses play themselves out in the media and in popular culture. Those that do not speak, or dare not speak out of fear and ignorance, remain powerless behind the walls created by their own limited perception. You can be equally proud of where you come from as you are proud of where you currently find yourself. Pride is not the property of a physical place. Pride is also not the monopoly of the political elite. Pride is rather an internal awareness of your true worth and the connection you possess to and with a power greater than yourself.

Pride was important for our ancestors because often, after being stripped of land, wealth and power, pride in heritage and identity was the most valuable principle and commodity to leave as a heritage for the children. Taking pride in your heritage can provide a source of identity and a connection to the important lessons of the past. These lessons which emphasize balance, harmony and the ability to connect directly to the universal power of creation, still have as much relevance and applicability today as they did thousands of years ago.

Express your pride with gratitude. Your achievements are not merely your own accomplishments. Your unique talents and abilities were specifically designed and developed within the mind of the Creator. There is a message and a purpose that only you can express. There is a divine message that seeks expression through your life. If you listen carefully, if you pay attention to your likes and talents, that unique message will make itself known. Be proud of all those people who contributed to your success and be proud that now you are their representative. Your success is the collective success of all those who have touched your life.

Lesson: Defend What Is Yours

Pride lies in knowing who you are, where you come from and what you stand for. Don't allow anyone to instill shame in you by telling you that you are inferior to others because of your background or origin. You are a child of nobility, of fierce warriors, wise rulers and powerful healers. This is a rich legacy which certainly gives you the privilege and full rights to pride and honor. Being proud of your origins and your heritage does not make you a braggart. It does not make you ungrateful to this great nation that is now your home. You can be doubly proud to represent two cultures because you know your history and you know the contributions your family has made to defend such organizing principles as freedom, equality, justice and peace.

Fight for what you believe with a confidence of your place in the great cosmos. Defend those you care for with a clear conviction of your values and ideals. Be proud of your place here and now. This is the place you have earned in life. In this place, everything you dare imagine can be possible. This is the place carved out for you by those who dreamed and hoped for your greatest achievements. You have worked hard and have overcome many obstacles; know that greater things still await you.

Lesson: Affirm the Positive

If you want to be happy and feel that your life is unfolding according to your greatest potential, you must become aware of the critical and damaging thoughts you retain as truth. These false myths are creating a world of suffering. You can improve your life by becoming aware of these damaging thoughts and you can set up a plan to systematically erase them from your mind.

The first step is becoming aware. Learn to tune in to the constant dialogue that goes on in your head. Listen to the thoughts and catch yourself s you say critical and damaging things. Some people find it useful to put a rubber band around their wrist and snap the rubber band whenever they catch themselves entertaining a negative thought. Another exercise might involve journaling and keeping a written record of the negative thoughts, when they happen and the circumstances under which these thoughts occur. Journaling gives you a great ability to see patterns over a period of time. Becoming aware of complex thought patterns can show you connections that may not be readily apparent.

These exercises can increase your ability to be mindful and can heighten your awareness while helping you to identify areas where further work might be needed. Repeat the false thought to yourself and replace it with an affirmation of what you know to be true. For example, you might catch yourself saying something critical like, "I am never going to be happy because I'm too scared to change." Replace the damaging thought with an affirmation of the truth by saying something like, "I know that happiness is my divine inheritance. I know that happiness is possible right here and now and I know that fear is simply a lack of awareness. I know I am divinely supported and all I need to do is be willing to take the first step."

You might want to start your day with a daily affirmation. This practice can help set the tone for a positive and constructive attitude than can last all day. Try to practice remaining aware of the moment as it unfolds. Meditation is a great way to increase awareness. Practicing mindful meditation will increase your ability to recognize false and damaging thoughts as they occur. Learn to stop yourself the moment you entertain a damaging thought and replace the thought with the affirmative truth. In a short amount of time, you will feel more energized and optimistic.

9

Happiness is at Hand

Congratulations, you have already taken several steps towards living a more joyous and prosperous life. You have decided to be happy and have committed yourself to staying open to the many options life offers. You must make the changes that will support your new commitment. You don't need to know every detail of what must come next, nor do you need to eliminate the fear and uncertainty you might feel right now. All you are asked to do is believe that you are being supported by the love that has been carefully transferred from a rich ancestral past. Such love has been laid for you to discover and if you but take one step in the right direction all of your efforts will be handsomely rewarded. The fear and uncertainty you might feel right now will disappear as you begin to embrace your new awareness.

Your mind already contains all the tools needed for this journey of self discovery. Your mind is a fertile ground and through the thoughts that you plant on that ground, you will be able to transcend the ordinary bounds of existence. You are an agent of change. United with that power, you can direct your mind and become an active participant in the co-creation of your world and your reality. Your mind focuses on certain experiences while it ignores others. What enters into your field of knowledge is a composite of the factors and events which your mind has retained and has held as truth. Yet these factors and events, which occur in your mind, represent only a fraction of what is actually going on in the universe of infinite possibilities. What you don't perceive is so much greater and more powerful than the small, insignificant amount of stimuli you can actually perceive.

It is through the awesome transcendence of our minds and the receptivity of an open heart that we can perceive and obtain an understanding of the divine. The divine, the Creator, the grand ancestors, the higher seat of consciousness, all of these terms represent a poor attempt to describe the awesome power of what cannot be described. Yet, there are those who have tried to market and sell even the power of the Divine. Across time and throughout the world, the human mind has been controlled precisely through the manipulation of the Divine. In the name of God, millions have been murdered or subjected to servitude and suffering.

As the human mind evolved across the ages, it increased its awareness and understanding of the connection it holds to the infinite universal laws of creation. We have increased our understanding of the mind and know that the force behind our thoughts is the same power our ancestors called the Divine Creator. God and mankind are intricately connected, serving as a mirror and as an expression of one to the other.

One of the greatest mysteries of the human experience occurs when we contemplate how we are able to know and understand the power that gives us awareness. The contemplation of that mystery is humanity's first interaction with the invisible power of creation and its Creator. You look towards the divine to transcend your reality because your mind naturally reaches beyond the realm of the tangible and limited world. Intuitively, you know you are so much more than the sum of your circumstances. Something inside you aspires for greatness and never ceases to reach forward, no matter what limitations are placed before you.

There is a close and personal connection that you feel between your concept of God and your own concept of yourself. You understand that you have free choice and as such, you participate in the co- creation of your own reality. You cannot continue to sit by the sidelines waiting for a miracle to happen in your life or waiting for God to deliver you from your oppression. You must take decisive steps to change your own life. Recognize that all you need to live the life you always thought possible is already available and laid out before you. You must have the courage to start upon the path intended for you. You must, at the same time, be willing to let go of all those things and ideas which, while they might have provided you comfort and familiarity, also held you back.

Contrary to what you might have been taught, you don't have to wait to die in order to go to heaven. The kingdom of heaven is at hand. Happiness and joy are abundantly available here and now. Dare to imagine the life you wish to live and allow your thoughts to impact and influence the power of creation. The promise of the Fifth Sun, the promise of enlightenment, joy and liberation is being fulfilled through you. When you walk in line with your intended path, when you pay attention to the messages the ancestors left as your inheritance, you will discover the significance of one of their greatest teachings. *There is no death. There is no end. There is only one life unfolding eternally and expressing itself as your very own life.*

The legendary journey and search for home has been illustrated by our ancestors; but today, the search for peace and permanency, the search for self discovery, takes place in the mind. Your birth, the birth of your identity, and the transformation to your highest self are really steps that have been labeled by the ancestors to guide your way. The steps below outline the process that occurs as one previous identity gives way to a higher awakening.

Step One: Genesis
Task: Start with a Complete Self Assessment

The myths of our ancestors tell us that creation began with an idea or a word. The Creator had to give birth in order to be Creator. You are a child of that strong desire to create. Within you, genesis represents the birth of your awareness; the birth of a conscious thought directed towards creation. From this awareness, you will begin a journey that leads you to an even greater level of self realization. The voyage of self discovery always leads back to you; but in the introspection process, you obtain a higher degree of awareness regarding the nature and quality of the choices you make.

Every second of your life, you are presented with an opportunity to choose. The moment of choice occurs during the split second between an event as it unfolds and your reaction to it. Your identity, the concept you have of yourself, is determined the moment you choose between two or more options of reality. As an example, you may be driving to a family party. Depending on the concept you hold of yourself in relation to your family, you will either be excited to go or you will dread every step of the way. Your thoughts enter a room before you do and they set the stage for the reality you will live. Your life is made up of the decisions and the choices you have made. To be happy, you must trace back your past; recognize how some of your decisions were made with limited or false information, forgive and move into an unburdened present.

Start the journey of self discovery by conducting an assessment of your life. Examine your family history and determine your place within that system. Look at family patterns and how different family members might have played different roles, perhaps of heroes and villains and then identify how these patterns might still influence your present life. Identify the dreams and the false myths and teachings you have integrated. It is easier than you might think. Remember that the core of who and what you are is divine perfection, untouched by human frailties. The negative thoughts and beliefs you have integrated must relate to a myth or false teaching you have incorporated as truth. The easiest way to complete this self assessment is to write down your life story or tell it into a recorder. Start in five year periods. What do you remember about your first five years of life? What about from the age of five to ten? What happened from ten to fifteen years of age? Continue in this way until you arrive to the present. Ask yourself how happy you were in each one of those five year cycles. Keep a score. You can use a scale from one to ten:

1   2   3   4   5   6   7   8   9   10
Very unhappy   Very happy

These scores are relevant only to you. If you consistently score low in every five year cycle of life, you might start asking yourself what was happening or not happening to cause you to be so unhappy then. What choices do you need to make today in order to begin to change these themes and myths that have created such unhappiness in your life?

You participate with the universe in the creation of your everyday reality. Everyday, you awaken to a new world and wipe the slate clean. While you can use your past as a teacher, you do not have to be burdened by repeating the same patterns. As the great artist, Ben Harper, sings, "Don't let your future be your past." With each passing day, you have the potential to come closer in contact with the full power and the full expression of the divine spark that dwells whole and complete within you.

The biblical creation myth states that when God first created the world, it was covered in darkness and confusion. If God is perfect, why would He not create a perfect world to begin with? Yet, if the world was created perfectly, how would we ever know to aspire to something better, something that more closely resembles the perfection of the divine? If all was perfect, what material would you use to transform yourself?

All of us are given challenges in life that allow us to test our mettle and our very essence. It is through these challenges that we are able to recognize who we are and what we believe. Most often, the more we struggle, the more we suffer. The more we recognize the perfection of the universe, the closer we come to understanding the complex wisdom and loving pattern of creativity. God takes pleasure, not in the completed process, but in the beauty of the imperfect in the process of transcending and becoming a closer reflection of the perfect. The Lost Sheep and The Prodigal Son are beloved and powerful myths because they demonstrate that we can find our way back from darkness and confusion. Your mind has the capacity to generate from seeming nothingness any idea that you plant and cultivate. Your mind duplicates the process of the creation of the world itself. From darkness and confusion comes order and structure. The dark gives way to the light. Confusion always gives way to clarity.

As you divide your life story into five year segments, you will begin to see patterns that keep occurring. Think about the primary figures in your life during each of the five year segments. What was your relationship like with your mother?

What about your father? How did you get along with your brothers and sisters and other significant relatives? What did you think about God? Everything that you have experienced before is useful and needed for your continued journey forward. It is never too late to change the course for the better. I have heard so many stories of people who say, "I know I am not happy, but I am too old to change." Or "I just don't want to go to all the trouble of changing my life. I have gotten so used to things the way they are, even if I am miserable."

Create a list of all the significant people in your life and the hurts and write down or record your thoughts about each. How did you feel about your elders and your cultural past? Did you feel cared for and protected? How did you react to difficult moments? Think about your answers and write them down or tell them into a recorder. Leave your answers alone for at least two days and walk away. Try to take your mind off the exercise and then come back to it later. Take another look at your answers and observe the patterns again. You will begin to see themes emerge. These are the themes that require your attention and work.

You are beginning to alter the script of your life and during this time of transition you are likely to feel awkward, but don't be afraid. Think about the concept of God you were taught and the concept of the personal Creator that truly resides at the center of your core. Think of the Creator as the force within that guides you towards happiness, goodness and abundance. Clearly, there is a great difference between the God of oppression which was taught to the ancestors and the God whose presence is personal, indwelling and who invites you to co-create this world as an equal participant. This is the Creator who sits on the throne of your mind, utilizing your thoughts to manifest the life you dare project. The Creator is not a power external to you. You can come to feel the power of the indwelling Creator in your moments of stillness and peace. This divine presence is manifested in all you think and do. The only judge there is, sits in the center of your consciousness. This is the liberating and empowering Creator that knows only love and forgiveness and knows nothing of sin and punishment.

You have a right, as a child of the Fifth Sun, to adore a god that is manifested in your image. There is no God of the oppressor and no God of the oppressed. There is no accurate history which can rightly portray you as inferior while calling others the chosen. You have a right to see yourself reflected in the history of the world and in the celebration of life, not as a second class citizen, but as an empowered participant in the human story of evolution which is also the story of evolution of the divine. You have the same god given right as does everyone else to live according to your view of love and happiness. Think of yourself as a spokesperson and representative of the ancestral force of creation. You call the shots!

That does not mean that everything goes and that there is no moral or ethical compass by which you are guided. Don't fear that listening to your internal guide will lead to a life of abandonment and hedonistic living. There is a compass which is imbedded deep within you and which functions just as well today as when you were born. It is up to you to learn to read that compass as it whispers its gentle directions and its ancient wisdom.

Somewhere along the way so many native children have been misguided and mis-educated to trade their personal power for the pre-packaged notion of inferiority. These ideas, with their references to colonization, slavery, oppression and other myths of inequality, sell a view of inadequacy that continues a long history of unequal treatment. Yet, that mistreatment cannot last forever if you follow the path of your heart's desire. Light always breaks through the darkness. Eventually the veil of confusion is lifted and you see glimpses of your greatness. Every now and then you may see pictures of your life lived in accordance with the intention and potential you know is within you. Follow these glimpses and you will create a heaven on earth and realize your most cherished desires.

Step Two: Naming
Task: Identify Where and How You Hurt

Soon after you were born, you were given a name. There were many factors that contributed to your naming, including consideration of ancestral history. The thoughts that your parents had about your name, their wishes and hopes, were transferred to you. By now you have recorded and traced back your personal story. You have identified areas of your life that might still be a source of pain and suffering and now you can move forward and begin to take action. You must take personal responsibility to change areas in your life that have made you unhappy. No matter how much you might have been hurt or victimized, nobody can take the responsibility to implement these changes other than yourself.

Make a list of the changes you would like to make. By making this list, you are naming your reality. If you have trouble naming what is bothering you, let your body and thoughts speak to you. Find a place where you can be quiet for fifteen minutes. Sit in complete silence, away from children, family and phones. Close your eyes and relax your whole body. Ask yourself, "Am I truly happy?" and notice how your body and mind react. If you feel tension in your stomach, for example, take notice. Does your stomach feel tight or irritated? Examine your thoughts. What comes to your mind? You might have a vague memory that may not make sense. Let images come to you, even if you don't know their significance. Slowly, as you

191

remain open and receptive to these faint messages, you will receive more and more signs from the past. Your willingness to stay open to the messages will increase the strength of the lost memory. You might choose to write down what you felt, saw and remembered.

Remember that being unhappy is an unnatural state. Life is a natural gift of awareness intended to be an expression of love and joy. Contrary to what you might have been taught, there is no honor or glory in suffering. There is no divine power that will reward your suffering and your postponement of joy. There is no purgatory or hell to which you will go if you don't obey. Heaven is not a place that awaits you as a reward after you have adequately denied yourself everything in life. Every moment of your life is eternal. Every moment of your existence you are presented with the opportunities to name your reality and to choose to act in accordance with your higher good. The results of your choices will become evident as patterns of behavior and will either increase the amount of good that comes your way or increase the amount of pain and suffering you endure.

As you increase awareness of your true nature, the false images of the self die away and melt into nothingness. What you do, what you contribute to others in love and kindness is returned to you many times over. The pain and suffering you endured are not intended as punishment for bad choices you've made. Instead, pain and suffering are instructive, appearing and reappearing in your life as feedback and opportunities for self correction. If you can break the secret language found in the patterns of your suffering, you can let go of the need to integrate pain and hurt as a regular part of your life. You can identify the door to eternity found in the stillness and peace of a deep meditation. Compare this tranquility to the turmoil caused by extreme changes which will always tend to drag you down.

Learn to detach from the transitory experience of suffering. Even when you feel that anxiety, loneliness and stress are consuming your life, take a breath. Tell yourself that these are hurtful thoughts manifesting in physical form. Perhaps they are old buried memories coming back to haunt you. These feelings may be traumatic fears of childhood which have nothing to do with your life today. Your body can get used to reacting as though it were in present danger, when in reality, the danger or threat may have been absent for years. Breathe deeply and know that all is well.

If your body is tense and you feel shortness of breath, take a second to recognize the thoughts you are entertaining. Say what you are thinking out loud. Can you identify the irrational thought? Replace the negative thought with a positive affirmation and breathe again.

It is in these moments of detachment from the anguish of pain and suffering that you receive glimpses of the divine peace and intelligence at your core. In these moments you recognize that the fear and anxiety you may be feeling can disappear under your direction. Talk to that unpleasant feeling as if it were a friend. You might say something like, "I know you are scared and I know you feel lonely, but I promise you I won't leave you." Notice how the tension begins to decrease. Reward yourself whenever you begin to feel the slightest improvement of your symptoms. You can stop the mental runaway train that threatens your peace. Notice how your own behavior and your own thoughts play out in such a manner that can either increase your heaven or perpetuate your hell.

Somewhere in the infinite continuum of space and time your actions, your choices and your decisions continue to live and reverberate for eternity. Each action, each choice that you make has a direct impact, not just on your life and on the lives of those around, but also on the rest of creation.

All of us are connected through this experience called life. All of us project and react to the world based on our images and thoughts of the power of creation, of the divine and of what we believe to be possible. Your sense of self and the ancestral collective histories impact everyone you meet. It is up to you to reach beyond the divisions created by history, oppression and perceived inequality. It is up to you to determine that these teachings are false. It is up to you to live your life according to the highest principle of truth that resides deep within you.

Although the external world may teach inequality, injustice and hate in all its varied forms, you must hold firm to your knowledge that what is acted out by those who hoard and fear is only a result of ignorance and mis-education and in no way represents the truth of who you are or the truth of your divine existence on this earth. You are here on this earth to deliver a message and to increase the amount of love, truth and happiness which generates from you and to you. Don't become caught up in the false teachings or in the appearance of a fabricated world of forms and objects. The popular culture will often demand your allegiance and indoctrination into a system that insists on placing your worth below that of so many others. Hold on to that part of yourself that does not change. Celebrate your divine origin, give thanks on a daily basis and let your greatness come forth in all its radiant glory.

Think about the barriers that have gotten in the way of your dreams and happiness. Why have these barriers remained as long as they have? What would it take to have these barriers removed? Reconnect to your ability to experience happiness and joy.

Write down the changes you would like to see happen on a sheet of paper. Maybe you would like to start a photography class or a fitness program. Under each goal, identify the steps that you should take to reach your desired outcome. Think about a realistic time frame. Create a plan of forty days, for example. The period of forty days not only has spiritual significance, but it also represents enough time to alter any old behavior pattern. Stay committed and consistent to your plan for the forty days.

After the forty days are over, analyze your goals again and evaluate your progress. How did you do? Congratulate yourself. Acknowledge your efforts and hard work. If you did not fully achieve your desired goal, don't beat yourself up. Recognize what was accomplished and re-evaluate your progress. Maybe you confronted some barriers that you had not previously identified. What thoughts did you have while working on your goals? Were you able to stay optimistic, or did you begin to feel thoughts of doubt and failure? Keep track of these thoughts, name them, recognize their genesis and learn to replace these negative myths with true affirmations. Revise your goals and the steps required to obtain your desired outcome; acknowledge and reward your work. Stay focused and committed. Very soon you will reach whatever goal you set for yourself.

Your mind is capable of tapping into the universal source of all intelligence and all knowledge, if you but listen to the hidden messages in the silence. You do not need anyone or any group to act as your advocate or your mediator to that source of knowing. It is time to link up directly. You need not be a follower of any specific dogma in order to recognize that you are connected to the creative power and intelligence which has brought everything into existence. Jesus, one of the greatest teachers of the true power of the mind, followed that voice with unwavering faith and conviction.

Ask yourself what you believe. What are the unspoken assumptions you make about your life, your purpose, your direction? Take these questions and examine their personal significance. Even if you do not believe in God, it is good for you to have an exploratory dialogue with yourself addressing the existential questions of your place and purpose on this planet. Whatever conclusions you develop are correct because they are correct for you. Open yourself up to hear the voice of your consciousness. There is an endless treasure buried within your mind and that treasure will guide you to realize your life's potential. You are a vital component of the creative process. You stand as a necessary witness to this experience called life. Your testimony is valued and required. Your unique voice adds the necessary and logical chapter in the continued book of creation.

Step Three: The Break
Task: Understand the Law of Desire

During this step of your journey, you are asked to review what you once felt you knew. You will often be confronted with a break between your previously held notion of reality and your new awareness. You may realize that you have been harboring anger towards your parents for years. The new awareness already represents a break from your previous notions. Allow yourself to feel the disillusionment and disappointment, but don't stay in the pain. Your disillusionment can get you stuck, or it can prepare the ground needed to evolve to a higher level of awareness.

Your specific vibration is like no one else's and it includes verbal and non-verbal behavior, body language, emotions and so much more than the physical senses are able to perceive. You can't hide who you are. In one moment you give away many clues to your state of mind. Likewise, you are able to pick up as many clues and messages when first meeting someone new. There are feelings and strong reactions you get the moment you meet someone. While you might not know how to describe what you sense, your mind is picking up and processing a great deal of information.

The external world responds to your internal state of equilibrium. You contribute greatly to whatever is physically manifesting in your life. You tend to believe however that it is your environment which determines your internal state. If you feel a void inside of you, for example, you tend to find the external means of satisfying that void. Sex, drugs, money, food, whatever you perceive to be lacking, you pursue single-mindedly. The more you pursue these physical agents of satisfaction and temporary escape, the more dissatisfied you will become with your life. You are seeking to name a void that cannot be satisfied with any external source. You pursue your source of pleasure like an obsessed lover pursues an indifferent love object. The more you pursue your external source of pleasure, the more you become enslaved by your desires. It is not entirely your fault. This consumer driven society tells you that if you are feeling an internal void, you must take something, buy something, eat something or have someone fill that void. As a result, you are left always in consuming mode, always reaching for more and never feeling satisfied. You become like the Tibetan hungry ghosts, *pretas*, in hell with their huge stomachs and tiny mouths, unable to eat to satisfy their huge hunger.

By believing in an unobtainable model, you instantly become dependent on the pursuit and, in the process, consume all that you think will make you happy. If you are comparing the sex you are having to the sex people are having in the *novelas* and in the movies, you will inevitably feel the whole world is having a great time and you are being left out. The drama of the movies and *novelas* takes you to a world so much more interesting and glamorous than your own. Everyone is beautiful and hypersexual. You look at the beautiful people and want to live their life instead of yours. Suddenly you find yourself chasing an impossible image. You are chasing that specimen of perfection and are always comparing yourself negatively and critically in the process.

Desire multiplies itself upon desire. The best sexual experience, for example, often leaves you wanting to experience that rush once again. You create a memory out of a one time peak experience, and you hold on to that memory as the measure for all other subsequent experiences. What you are holding on to, in this example, is not just that great sexual experience, but in your mind, there is a process of embellishment. Your mind recalls peak experiences because they are so out of the norm. It becomes very difficult for your mind to be content with the stable, middle ground. Your mind remembers the best experience ever imaginable and demands greater and greater satisfaction because it is looking for greater meaning in the experiences. Even if it were possible to re-experience that same sexual encounter with the same person and the same intensity, it would not be as fulfilling as you think you remember. The more you chase, the more you feel that emptiness.

Sex, drugs, alcohol, food, and countless other addictions, can only provide temporary relief, but they trick the brain chemically, so that the brain wants more and more to feel the same temporary relief and sense of fulfillment. It becomes impossible to ever satisfy that void with any substance or any person. The emptiness must be dealt with from the foundation. This is the central makeup of any addiction. By holding on to peak experiences, you unsuccessfully seek to duplicate that same exhilaration time and time again. You try being in the same place, surrounded by the same people, but nothing ever seems to get you to that elusive ecstasy.

When you are unable to replicate what you are searching for, you become disappointed with life itself because life no longer seems to meet your expectations. Your definition of pleasure has become so narrow that it must match the peak experience you seek, but that peak experience never existed. Your mind was tricked into believing the altered chemical state was true happiness. Your search intensifies and you become more dissatisfied. This great inner void, this inability to feel fully satisfied, is placed there by the Creator. This great emptiness is meant to be there, because it is the only way you can understand the infinite potential and boundless nature of the infinite. The only way to fill that void is to engage directly and internally with the source of your consciousness as an attempt to relate to the infinite.

The fulfillment of the promise of the Fifth Sun will take place in the most revolutionary and most fertile grounds in the universe -- your mind. The chaos and confusion that typifies the creation myths all over the world, is the symbolic representation of your mind in a state of disorder and darkness. When thoughts of regret, lack of worth, fear, anger and resentment are allowed to fill your mind, your external world responds with similar confusion, chaos and problematic relationships, mirroring the chaos in your mind. There is a collective mind, a universal voice that is yours to use as you need. Hear it by calming the chatter around you. No matter how uncertain your individual life becomes, if you look deep within yourself, you will come to tap into the wisdom of the collective ancestral mind and the internal voice of the higher self. This is the inner voice that contains the truth of our existence.

Peace and happiness arrive when you are able to discipline your mind. Order and structure begin to take hold when you are able to manage your thoughts and heighten your awareness. Control your thoughts and you will be able to calm the stormy seas. When you confront your demons, when you take control of your mind, you will bring about the rising of the Fifth Sun within you and you will step into your divine inheritance. In order to bring about the reign of the Fifth Sun, you must be willing to experience the death of the old world. This is no easy task, since the world you have built is full of familiar comforts. This is the ultimate sacrifice you are being called to make. You must be willing to open your heart and lay it upon the high altar of the ONE God and step bravely into your personal transformation. You must be willing to calm the tempest and separate the darkness and chaos of your world, calling forth and speaking your word with confidence and authority, proclaiming: "Let there be light." You must be willing to experience the death of your old self so that you may rise and be reborn to your true power.

It has taken many years to arrive where you are today, so be patient if the changes that you desire don't happen overnight. A commitment to happiness and fulfillment is still a commitment. To change any pattern of behavior requires discipline and consistency. You must be willing to make a life change and must let go of past behaviors, routines and harmful elements that you have held out of a false sense of security and safety.

There might be moments when the newness feels uncomfortable and to avoid the discomfort, you might be tempted to retreat. You have a protective mechanism that makes you flinch at pain and retreat from danger. It is a natural human reaction. You either stand up to fight, or you run away from the danger. Yet, this survival mechanism can also be tricked by repeated exposure to trauma and stress. Your mind can fall into a pattern and can react out of habit even when the danger is long gone.

The mind can be redirected if it is reminded that the danger is gone. If you identify how these patterns of behavior developed and how these reactions were once helpful, you can then redirect your mind to better react to the present. Since the danger is long gone, you no longer need your mind to protect you in the same manner it once did. Give thanks that your mind was once able to protect you and determine to move beyond the habitual and impulsive reactions. You are not alone and you never have been. We all share in this experience called life. Transforming your life by transforming your thoughts is a challenge that will inevitably bring you face to face with the past and with the painful memories you might have avoided until now.

Step Four: The Journey Itself
Task: Examine Your Personal Myth and Identity

No matter how painful or dissatisfied you may be with your present life, it is never too late to change your direction. A critical part in changing directions is learning to identify the areas that have gotten you stuck in the past. Learning to name your monsters and your fears is an essential part of being able to destroy what frightens you. Lack of experience in properly labeling and naming emotions can cause you to have an inability to recognize when such emotions begin to invade your mind.

The process to obtain a higher level of awareness represents the mythical journey from paradise. Out of paradise, out of that place of ideals, innocence and peace, you are thrown into a wilderness or into an arid desert of lack, fear and confusion.

The journey requires movement. You don't have to feel you have the energy to run a marathon, but you have to be willing to take the next step forward and trust that, each step of the way, the road will be made clear for you. Make a commitment to your happiness.

It may be easy to identify with what you don't like and what you don't want, but it may actually be more difficult to think about what you DO want. It may have been a long time since you thought about what would increase your joy, but it is never too late to start. The clearer you are about identifying those activities that you enjoy, the more likely you are to commit to following your bliss. Try something new and expand your horizons. When I was a child, I was convinced I hated olives. Why? They looked funny and were always hidden in food. I just knew I would hate them. I felt that, if they had to sneak into the food, they probably shouldn't be there at all. Then one day I tried one, then another. Today, I love olives and know that I always have. Where are your olives hiding? What experiences are you denying yourself because you are certain you would not like something or other? Sometimes you can make quick judgments that may end up closing you off to great possibilities. Remain open to what life has to offer and be willing to explore and experience something new.

You might want to create a list of all your dreams. This list of dreams represents your revised map which is necessary to continue along the correct path. Be as detailed as possible. Find a friend you trust and let them know your desires. Often, we think that we have to keep our dreams to ourselves for fear they may not come true, but if you have people you trust to share your hopes and aspirations, you will actually find support in reaching your goals. Don't allow for life's ups and downs to discourage you from your dreams.

Part of learning to adequately identify your emotional state is to identify the feelings and beliefs you have attached to your personal myth. Your individual myth is soaked in the emotions you've given to your story. You are attached, not only to your individual story, but also to the distant memories of feelings you've developed about your story: your recollected pain, your anger, your sadness. You hold on to all of the emotions you have experienced, believing that you are this pain and that suffering. Emotions have a way of making you feel that a given situation is solid and permanent. There is no doubt that life will place speed bumps in your path. While you may be unable to avoid heartbreak and loss, you do have a choice on how to react. When heartbroken, allow yourself to experience the hurt, grief and agony, but also look for the lesson and the gift behind the experience. Remember that disillusionment is often a necessary step towards obtaining a broader understanding. If you keep your heart open, you will find that behind every loss there is always a great lesson and a gift that remains.

If you stay attached to your pain, you will develop a false belief that you are your past. Because you are focusing on your pain, you are only able to trace back the route of suffering and are not capable of looking further back to your grand beginnings and to the original glory of your ancestry. Soon you identify yourself as the oppressed, "los de abajo" (the ones below) and it becomes increasingly difficult to feel empowered and capable of impacting your world. Be determined not to live in the past and be determined to see things just as they are. Make a turning point today and change your life for the better. As the great Cesar Chavez stated, "Si se puede!"

This moment of your personal commitment marks with significance your date of rebirth. From this day forth, you vow to turn away from what you know is the wrong direction. You will turn towards what you know to be your intended path. Be ready for all that change brings along with it. Be ready to say goodbye to old habits and to people who have lingered but are not really your friends. Be prepared as you change your life to encounter criticism by many individuals and institutions that may not understand or agree with you. Let the universe take care of the details and don't allow yourself to be distracted by apparent setbacks and disappointments. Think of these apparent bumps in the road as small clues and revelations, put in your path to help you stay committed to your vision and dreams. Maintain your focus on your desires, dreams and aspirations and in time, the thought and effort you put forth will convert your dreams into your reality.

Step Five: Reclaiming/Rebirth
Task: Walking the Path

You have committed yourself to walk the path of your true potential and identity. It is the path that was intended for you by the Creator and the ancestors. This path is lived from an awareness of universal principles which are impersonal, but which can be used to enrich your life. These principles are teachings that emphasize the relationship with all elements of creation. Trace back the ancestral past and view your life from the dreams and aspirations of the past. You are the reason for the promise made. You are what the ancestors envisioned when they built the pyramids and projected their hopes for a greater future. Uncover the sacred code of your intention. Uncover the unique purpose of your life, uncover your *tonalli* and live your life with purpose and intention.

This step involves exercising control over your own destiny and standing firm, reclaiming what you felt was once lost or taken from you. You are complete. Nothing that has ever happened to you has broken your spirit. Now you can drop the excess baggage, lighten your load and be born into a heightened state of awareness. As you start on your path, commit to begin each day with a few moments of silence. Before you rush out to meet the busy day, spend a few minutes by yourself. Listen to the silence and clear your mind. Set your intention for the day. Imagine the type of day you will have. Picture the people you will see and the opportunities that will present themselves to you. Breathe deeply and affirm your connection to the wisdom of the ancestors. Ask the universe and the ancestors for guidance and support and tell yourself what you wish to accomplish for the day. You will witness the power of your own thoughts as you begin to actively and consciously project your intention onto every day.

Although, at first it may be difficult to stay focused and keep your mind clear, with practice you will find that you are able to increase your concentration and the amount of time you are able to sit still. Fight the thoughts that say you have not achieved enough; you have not tried hard enough. Ironically, the harder you try the harder it is to get out of this rut and rat race. The only answer to this problem may seem ironic and contradictory, but it is to be still. Stop trying so hard and let it all go. Reconnect to that deep sense of purpose that was present even before the moment of your birth. Reclaim the treasure that is rightly yours and keep yourself light and happy. The process of self discovery should be fun and creative, not drudgery. If you feel weighted down, you are heading in the wrong direction. If you work with purpose and intention, the work will seem effortless and fun, not a burden. You are worthy and you are complete -- just as you are -- without having to try any more.

You can no longer afford living in fear. Fear of others will only lead to retaliation against a perceived enemy. We must all learn to break free from our oppressive personal history. The victim must rise up. The resentful must forgive. The fearful must see the light of truth. All of us must step away from our personal injury and pain. Learn to view the pain of your past through a positive and transformative lens. How has your suffering contributed to making you the strong, sensitive person you are today? What have you learned about yourself and others? We've all suffered the effects of colonization, hatred and social injustice and now it is time for us to heal our world collectively. In order for us to do this we have to reach out in compassion and empathy to our brothers despite any apparent differences. Regardless of our background and cultural heritage, we have to be willing to have the difficult dialogues and hear with an open heart the experiences of the other.

You have the power to transform the entire planet by transforming your own reality. The injustices of a society won't be healed by waiting for someone else to realize that change is necessary. You must be that agent of change. You must live your life according to the internal principles which guide you without being concerned about what the external world does in response. In other words, live your life! Don't be too concerned with what other people are or are not doing. Living a life in line with your intention is the best way to impact the world. Determine what you are called to do and do that! Finding your intention is easy if you are able to turn the volume down on the surrounding chaos to listen to your own inner voice.

The promise of the Fifth Sun states that the end of the world is near, but it is not an Armageddon or end of the physical world. It is, rather, the end of life as you have known it and the promise of awakening to a new life, governed by the light of a new sun of self awareness and enlightenment. It is awakening to the Fifth Sun and to the light that has always been shining inside you. When you connect to that inner source of life and energy, you will discover your connection to all of creation. You will be guided by the ancestral teachings which can never lead you astray and which will always guide you gently towards your happiness. It is time to awaken to a different reality and to begin to live from this deeper knowing.

To stay connected to that inner voice and intuition, you must live as the ancestors once did and strive to be in balance with all elements. Eat right, exercise and don't drink or use drugs excessively, because such extremes depress your system and cause emotional imbalances, such as depression and anxiety. Balance your recreational and work time and don't be too concerned about your future. Tomorrow will reveal itself in time, if you just maintain your dreams and keep your aspirations alive.

As you begin to re-discover your ancestral past, you will also become increasingly aware of the deep connections you have to others. If you trace your family's history far enough, you will find that we are all "parientes" and "compadres". We are descendents of a family that has survived millions of years of immigration and migration in search for the lands of freedom and equality, abundance and peace. We are all called to create a new myth for an integrated world. Today you are called to reach beyond your individual history. Each one of us is asked to step back from our individual perspective of pain and recognize our connection to the global family. The mythology we create as a global community must be the inclusive myth of a new age. This powerful new cosmic myth is one of transcendence and enlightened awakenings. This new story shows the path of transcendence from physical limitations to the unbound potential of creation. You inhabit a universe much more expansive and interactive than you ever imagined.

Turn towards the greater power which transcends the limits of a material world. All power comes from the ONE source. The source that gives all power is fully aware of your potential. The source of this power awaits your decision for personal liberation. The limitations which you perceive exist only in your mind.

The face of the Fifth Sun sits in the center of the Aztec Calendar ever still amidst the change, the ebb and flow of the material world. Tonatiuh, the God of the Fifth Sun, shows you the way. In order to awaken to the eternal world, you must be willing to make a conscious decision to let go of your pain and suffering. Your joy waits patiently, wondering when you will open the door to let inside that which is your good. Your life is a search for meaning and a search for lasting happiness. This search is the search for the light of the Fifth Sun, the light of self revelation, awakening and enlightenment. The myths of your ancestors offer a deeper and more meaningful awareness of your existence on this earth. Myths are the psychological and cultural blueprints showing your connection to the everlasting life. Myths bring the ancestral past into present focus, while offering a window to the eternity of an infinite universe.

Step Six: Homecoming
Make a Daily Commitment to Happiness

Every journey ends in a homecoming of sorts. All of us are immigrants in unknown and often hostile lands. At some point, tired and weary from our search, we long for home. Mexicans, for example, identify strongly with the collective experience of the desire to return home. One of the unofficial Mexican national anthems is the song "Volver", which means to return. It is not, however, a return that we should seek, but a homecoming. A return will have us looking back. A homecoming allows us to look forward, recognizing that although the home we left may long be gone, it is not the physical structure or the specifics we are searching for, but it is the knowing that, wherever we are, we know that we have been guided there by a loving wisdom that wishes us joy, peace and happiness. We must all, at some point, make a personal decision to be happy, despite our past. Who are you when it is just you and your thoughts? Don't you hear the voice of your ancestors telling you that you are the reason for the sacrifice? You are a brother of the earth and a sister of the heavens. Your ancestors have entrusted you with the greatest treasure found within the universe. This is the treasure that assures your connection to all of life. The secret of eternal life is bestowed upon you as you recognize the ever changing illusion of the material world.

Every moment of life is a moment of choice. If you have somehow been rewarded for thinking negatively and have focused on what you lack, you must now hold back from that tendency. Keep all your options open and when given the opportunity, think of the highest and best possible outcome before giving in to the negativity. Your happiness should be your first priority. If you prioritize your happiness, your heart will grow and soon you will have an incredible amount of compassion for others as well.

It is only because you know truly where love resides, that you can give it away. In order for you to be able to give love away, you must feel yourself complete. It is only when you are satisfied with yourself that you can find greater satisfaction in loving everything and everyone around you. You are not trying to grab or influence, but rather, you are a grateful observer of an expanding awareness. You become love itself. Whatever you behold magnifies and becomes who you are.

When something happens that you instantly feel might be negative, hold off judging the experience. Learn to look at any situation through several possibilities. As an example, if someone you like does not call, don't assume that they don't like you. So often, we are taught to hope for the best, but prepare for the worst. That teaching is really damaging and impossible for the mind to entertain. If you are preparing for the worst, your thoughts and actions are focused on the negative outcome. You may say that you are hoping for the best, but in reality, you doubt that the best will ever come your way and so all you are left with is the worst possible outcome. Learn to catch yourself in the middle of a negative though and instantly replace that negative thought with a more positive possibility. Remember that the possibility for happiness occurs with every opportunity to decide. Make a daily commitment and decide with the highest possible outcome in mind. Your daily commitment to happiness will soon yield the abundance you deserve.

There are difficult discussions that we must be willing to have in order to heal the many wounds of the past. Whether you feel you have profited from this collective history of colonization or whether you feel that you have been victimized by the segregated hatred, you are cheated out of the greater experience for deeper human connection. You cannot stay quiet about your pain and suffering, nor can you continue to feel guilty or coldly indifferent to the experiences of injustice and inequality suffered by others. You cannot stand by and see the divisions which silently split people into sectors of fear and isolation.

Homecoming includes not just a selfish notion that your life is better, but improving your personal life is a requirement for everything else. Homecoming implies a unity and a connection to others. Hearing someone's experience and becoming tolerant of the embedded pain and suffering endured is the cornerstone of true understanding. This is the healing that our human experience requires in order for us to come together in love. Looking at life through polarities of right and wrong, good and bad will make you inflexible and intolerant. It is a greater challenge to recognize the presence of all in us all. It is a greater challenge to recognize our human history as a collective experience and collective inheritance.

Step Seven: Unification
Task: Forgive and Let Go

The final step on the journey towards a higher sense of awareness and a higher consciousness is not even a step, but a sudden realization that the destination has been reached. This step often sneaks up because, while you have been busy moving and trying to get someplace, eventually, you come to rest and as you do, you can begin to look around and realize that everything you projected has become a reality. You are now in union with creation. In this step, you recognize that your word, your thought has manifested exactly what you desired. The vision that you fostered with faith has produced fruit. You now recognize that your word has power and that, when spoken with faith and confidence, it must manifest what you speak. As you recognize yourself as being one with creation, you no longer have the need to carry grudges or to hold on to any blame of the past. You open yourself up to the gift of forgiveness, of letting go.

The process of forgiveness liberates you and frees you so that you may be able to move and live in your true, higher nature. Often you don't allow yourself to forgive because you may feel that by forgiving you might somehow excuse what happened to you. You don't want to minimize the hurt and trauma you have suffered by pretending all can be forgotten. Yet resentment and anger, insult and injury keep you locked in misery. Forgiveness is about releasing yourself from held pain so that you can grow beyond the self imposed limitations created by holding on to old wounds. When you hold resentments, you clog yourself with regret and self pity. You hold the spirit of the one that harmed you captive; but more importantly, you also hold the growth of your own soul captive.

The process of forgiveness is also a process necessary to retain and resume control over your own life. Because no one can force you to forgive, choosing to do so allows you to reclaim a position of power. You retain power over your own life and you do not give any more power to those that have already injured you. Learning to forgive gives you control over situations that, at the time of your hurt, you felt you did not have.

As you begin to practice forgiveness, you discover that being insulted and personally injured is what leads you to hold resentments. You choose to interpret a given situation as personal when you believe that harm was directly intended for you. People cause injury most often because they act out of selfish motives, not out of a desire to harm. If you can recognize that everyone is doing the very best they can, if you can recognize that everyone is acting to secure their best interest, you can stop feeling so personally hurt. Just as you choose to feel insulted, you can choose not to react to your sense of disrespect and injury. If you begin to limit the number of situations and instances in which you take offense, you won't need to feel insulted and injured quite as often. Feeling hurt and injured is always your choice. If you decide to hold on to your feelings of hurt and anger, you will feel negativity dominating every element of your life. Learning to control the impulsive nature of your emotions is the greatest step towards evolution. Forgiveness restores the delicate balance and the harmonious flow of energy that is expressed through the manner in which you live your life.

Although forgiving others may be difficult, it is often even more difficult to forgive yourself. Those high expectations, for which you hold yourself painfully accountable, keep you from exercising kindness towards yourself and others. When you punish and blame yourself for all that has taken place in your life, you hold on to that experience and re-experience shame and guilt. Blaming yourself not only creates a barricade which prevents more pleasant experiences from entering into your life, but it also increases the likelihood that similar painful experiences will keep happening to you. Stop and recognize if you have made an error, apologize if you need to, but move on. Don't linger in the place of "I'm sorry, I didn't mean…, I feel so bad…, I can't believe…, I shouldn't have…" This is a quicksand trap. You cannot escape from this place, no matter how much you try. At some moment you must stop apologizing, get up off your knees and rise up. This is what Jesus meant when he said, "rise and sin no more". Simply put, if you are doing something that is bad for you, bad for your health, bad for your soul, stop it. Learn the lesson you are supposed to learn and go on with your life.

Lesson: Commit to Happiness

Happiness is possible but not always automatic. There are many people who have suffered greatly who still find it in their heart to choose happiness over despair. Yes, happiness is a conscious choice. You can allow yourself to be weighed down by the pain of your problems. Remembering and reliving your problems over and over, trying to find the fault in yourself or in someone else, can leave you heavy hearted and weary. There comes a time when you have to stop that senseless process and choose to be happy. All that you have experienced is valid, but there is also nothing you can do to change the past. Life waits for you, full and abundant. Embrace it! Claim it! I am amazed at so many "self-help" books that emphasize the pursuit of happiness. Happiness can sometimes feel elusive and if you can't get there, there are many "wellness" coaches that will get upset.   Happiness is possible, but it requires discipline, commitment and a willingness to accept change.

The first step in this process is to identify that you are unhappy. Sometimes, when you have only known suffering or lack, it is difficult to identify what this elusive "happiness" is supposed to look or feel like. People who have never experienced happiness may not know what happiness means.

Second, trace back the history of your family and ancestors. Take a look at their triumphs and their agonies. What are the stories they told? What were the ideals they fought for? How does your life fit into the overall pattern and design? Taking an inventory of your family system and ancestral heritage can give you the ability to step back and see the patterns imbedded in your collective heritage. Such perspective allows you to have greater control directing your life towards success and away from the pitfalls of past failures. Your suffering is often a result of your mind getting stuck attempting to solve some unsolved mystery. Once you identify these patterns of harmful thoughts and behaviors, you can set the intention to change them for thoughts and behaviors more consistent with happiness.   At each point where new awareness arises, old thoughts and the old behaviors will try to sneak back in. You must remain committed to change, even when stepping into new territory feels uncertain. When you feel yourself slipping back, stop yourself; recommit to your intention for happiness. Recognize that your happiness might need some definition. Look within and tap into your *tonalli*. What is the Creator's plan for your individual expression?

Consider this old Buddhist story that illustrates the process we undergo as we strive to obtain a heightened state of awareness.

I was walking down the street. There was a big hole. I did not see the hole and I fell in. The hole was deep and I did not know how to get out. I struggled for hours and hours, until exhausted; I finally gathered all of my strength and pulled myself out.

The next day, I was walking down the same street and fell into the same hole. I struggled for a while, but not as long as I did yesterday.

The next day I walked down the same street. I saw the hole and walked around it.

Today I am choosing to walk down a different road.

Be mindful and you will avoid repeatedly making the same mistakes. Be aware of not tripping over the same rock or falling into the same dark hole. Get your feelings and emotions out of the situation and analyze the patterns that begin to create automatic reactions without thought. Take a good look at those relationships and events that keep reoccurring in your life and learn what you must from the experience, but continue moving forward.

The process of falling down and getting up again is the manner by which we learn and develop the unique nature of our character. This is the journey of self discovery that eventually leads to unification with the universal power of creation. It does not matter how many times you fall. What does matter is how you address your predicament. Do you see your fall as a lesson or as a punishment? Free will allows you to trip upon the same stone however many number of times you need to trip. The kinder you are to yourself, the quicker you will learn the particular lesson required for your growth.

10

Welcome Home

The principle of leaving home is deeply imbedded in our psychological make-up. In order to find ourselves, we must leave the safety of the group and the comforts of home. The journey away from home is filled with adventure, danger, pleasure and temptation. Along the way, we grow and evolve; but at some point, we become weary of the travel and we long for the comforts and familiarity of a home to which we cannot return. This is the moment in which we are called to evolve. We must let go of the notions of the past and mourn the loss of what was; but at the same time, we must remain open to the greater possibilities of a fuller, more comfortable and more abundant version of home.

Leaving home represents a journey that is undertaken in search of your higher self. As you leave your place of comfort, you experience a profound tear in that fragile and precious concept of your "self", but you are rewarded handsomely as you evolve into a greater you. Like Jesus wandering in the desert, Buddha leaving his palace for poverty and the search of enlightenment, or our ancestors leaving Aztlan in search of Tenochtitlan, the journey of self discovery, by definition, tests your worth and it changes you in the process. By testing your limits and your capacity, you learn to go further than you previously thought possible. You find that the journey often brings you back to your beginning. The physical world may change drastically or hardly at all, but the greatest change lies in your own capacity to understand who and what you are. When you leave home, your family members may feel abandoned, as if you've bailed out on everyone and everything you used to be. Leaving home is leaving every thing that has ever been known as normal or comfortable in exchange for the experience of the greater unknown. Those of us leaving are likely to feel as though we are betraying our very nature and our very identity.

As the classic song asks:

"Cual de los dos amantes sufre mas penas, el que se va, o el que se queda. El que se queda se queda llorando y el que se va se va suspirando."

(Which of the two lovers suffers greater sorrow, the one who leaves or the one who stays? The one who stays, stays crying and the one who leaves, leaves sighing.)

The weary wanderer is always looking forward and when tired and discouraged, always stops to look backwards and in the process, misses the magic of the present as it reveals a new and more profound awareness. Time passes quickly, yet time is nothing but shadows dancing on the wall. If you focus on the shadows, you will miss the reality responsible for casting those shadows. Life changes and so does the world that once held our comforts and our sense of belonging. For many people living away from their homeland, it may be economically difficult or impossible to return home. Children grow up with little or no desire to return to an ancient land of their parents which is likely foreign to their own lives. This inability to return home tears at our hearts, making us, in essence, strangers in two lands and true citizens of none. Friends, relatives and acquaintances back home are likely to resent you for having ever left. They stayed behind to face the hardships while you may be perceived to have left for glory and wealth. The fabled land of "El Norte", where everyone's dreams come true, may seem to lie forever just out of reach.

Time and distance have a tendency to change everything, including your memory and recollection of events you believe are neutral. Your memories are not fixed or stable. They change as your attitude about present circumstances changes. Being unhappy and miserable in the present tends to make you more romantic about the past. The past is an illusion. No matter how hard you try; the past will never come back. Longing for the past will only distract you from building a happier life in the present. As you settle into a new home, everything will be unfamiliar and at first may seem more difficult. Nothing is as it was and as you seek a past that cannot return, you may come to doubt your own perception of reality. To protect yourself, you might withdraw and isolate yourself from others. This self isolation might give you a temporary feeling of safety, but in the long run, avoiding interactions with your environment will only make you more fearful and mistrustful.

Wherever you find yourself, learn to prosper and grow there. Learn to reach out to those around you and focus on what you can do for someone else. Focusing on the needs of someone else can remind you of your greater connection to everyone and can keep you away from painful self obsession. Stretch out your hand to someone who needs your help. Learn to care about someone else's troubles and you just might forget about your own for a while. Make this land your country and work to make it a better land for everyone. Make your current life your home and surrender to life. As you begin to accept life as it is, you will realize that it holds great beauty and magic that you might have missed before. Fight the urge to remain isolated and separated from the rest of the world. If you don't stretch yourself, you won't grow.

Learn to view your home as the place where the heart resides and not so much a physical location. Your eternal home is the peace found within your mind. The connection to the land and to your culture resides in your heart. You do not have to prove to anyone who or what you are. You are priceless and unique and your life was born out of the infinite wisdom of the Creator. So many times we insult each other based on our cultural identification and connection. Those that are first generation call those that are born here *pochos*, ridiculing them for not speaking Spanish. Those that are born here ridicule those that have arrived as *wetbacks*, or ignorant, without recognizing they only insult themselves. We are all children of a new America made strong by the present and historical contributions of so many committed citizens of diverse backgrounds and origins. We must learn to reach across the vague and arbitrary factors that divide us and reconnect to the oneness of our human family. It is in this reconnection and unification that we will find our true strength and identity.

The Meaning of Leaving Home

As sons and daughters of the Fifth Sun, you and I have often become wanderers in our own lands. That wandering is an instinct which propels you onward to wander this earth in search of that mythical place of peace, prosperity, joy and love because your mind and soul knows such a place truly exists. When it seems as though this heavy, sordid world of suffering and failure weighs upon your shoulders and it seems that you just don't belong, it is because your spirit holds a truth which is independent of all the maddening activity which surrounds you in the "real" world. Your spirit knows that within you there is an essence that is perfect, indestructible and all powerful. It waits patiently for you to tap into the realization of that power. You can tap into this infinite and complete essence by examining your thoughts and those behaviors which dilute your true potential.

Like your ancestors, you seek closeness to the land because you know and feel your deep connection to that living mother spirit which has always nurtured your needs. The history of your great ancestors is illustrated within the mythical, spiritual search that guided the journey from Aztlan to Tenochtitlan. The promise always propels you forward and guides you onward. Like the slaves out of Egypt, you are being lead to a promised land and the promise assures abundance, peace and goodness. Such a place exists untouched and unaltered, buried within your mind and the potential of your thoughts.

This is a literal and metaphorical search for a homeland. It is a search which promises the liberation of the oppressed and offers rest for the weary. This search for home is not just a search for the illusive lost lands romanticized and idealized by our hardworking relatives who have been immigrants, field and factory workers.

Home is also a search for the place of self actualization, the place where your full potential is realized. This place is found within the untapped regions and the endless potential of the human mind. You are the hero on a quest to reclaim the greatest treasure imaginable, yourself! You have often ventured into hostile lands, lost for many years in the desert of ignorance, temptation and self doubt. You have returned to the place of your beginning. Home is that place of inner peace that yields the riches you have awaited for so long. Home provides the long awaited rest resulting from the realization and the fulfillment of your sacred journey.

Through the long and painful experience of colonization, your ancestors have been bombarded with myths that specifically attempted to deconstruct and reconstruct a legacy of pride, culture and tradition. In Mexico City, there are numerous physical examples of this historic, systematic effort to bury a rich cultural past with the overwhelming power of a dominant subgroup. At the site of the most important spiritual centers of the native world, the colonizers destroyed and buried these sacred sites only to build new cathedrals on top of the graves of the past.

Disconnected from the roots of the past and moved by the power of self preservation, you are left wandering across borders like a homeless child looking for love and belonging. You and your ancestors have often been displaced out of homeland, forced to search for food and means of survival far from the land that saw your birth. In your mind still survives the collective myth of home as the lost paradise. You retain ancient memories of a time when you belonged to the land and not the other way around. You recall your greatness with a distant and melancholic yearning. The mistreatment you receive and the insults you absorb are an aberration of the truth. When it seems that there is no place where you belong, know that no amount of effort by any person, institution or circumstance could ever alter your true destiny. No external power could ever diminish your internal boundless source of power, peace and potential.

If you are compelled or forced to leave your home, you will feel torn from the familiar surroundings which give you a sense of comfort, stability and belonging. You may wander into far off lands feeling you no longer belong to the place you used to call home and you may often feel you cannot survive in the place where you now exist.

Displaced and uprooted, you live disconnected from the past and you are not available to the present. You work to create continuity and safety for your children and for others in your family, even if it means you sacrifice your own happiness in the process. Consumed by the urgency of surviving day to day, you cannot recognize that it is impossible to forgo your personal growth and happiness for the sake of someone else's well-being. No matter how much you do for others, it will never seem enough. No matter how much you hold others accountable, you will never feel fully restored. Live life emphasizing the importance of your own happiness and assume the responsibility for your own evolution and you will always feel your life expanding.

Don't allow fear, oppression and doubt to stop your progress and movement forward. Above all things, and despite all appearances, maintain your dream alive. Know that wherever you go, you are protected and supported on your journey. Our mother earth is imbued with spiritual significance and spiritual empathic support for your endeavors. It is a living organism with intelligence and it has a memory that is eternal. Our ancestors consecrated these lands with spiritual and psychological meaning. From the eagle devouring the serpent, to the building of sacred pyramids, to the upward stretching of mountains that forms a gateway to the ocean and an entry way into the heavens, these lands have a profound psychological significance and impact. These lands are infused with meaning, particularly for the wanderer who searches for self and home. Protective animal and human spirits are found everywhere and are available to guard your journey on this earth.

When you are most in need, trust that the right person and the right support will come into your life and provide you with all you require to move forward. Keep your eyes and attention focused on your ultimate goal and don't become discouraged.

Despite the poverty and despair that may have been your past, you long for a place to call home because your heart still recalls the abundant country of your origins. Be confident that the country and home you seek, the Promised Land of legends, still exists just as certainly as the sun rises every morning. Paradise is that place in your mind which is found when you come to know the infinite constructive and generative power of your thoughts. Learn to search for that home not just in the physical world, but within the wide open and fertile spaces of your mind.

Finding a place to rest and to prosper, a place to feel safe and a place to call home is a basic human drive shared by every citizen of this earth. The human soul knows nothing of man-made barriers and borders. Human existence has been defined by the search for food, shelter and safety. You do what must be done to secure the survival of your family and your loved ones. The creation of a stable home is your greatest and most cherished desire. If you are an immigrant, leaving the land that saw your birth is a deeply traumatic experience, the impact of which we've yet to understand completely. Your entire frame of reference changes and you no longer can be sure of many things. These trying times of change and transition require flexibility. You must learn to survive in a new, and often hostile, environment while maintaining a strong base rooted in a firm understanding of your core values and ideals. It is time to aspire to much more than simply survival. It is time that you reclaim the lost treasures of the past. All that you desire is yours if you simply believe.

Turn away from those people and experiences that do not serve you. These times of adaptation represent a most critical opportunity to draw from within your inner strength. During these trying times, however, you are most vulnerable and are likely to become distracted by all that is outside of you. As you encounter experiences and people that try to convince you that you are wrong, inferior or inadequate, you may become doubtful of even the most fundamental truth.

Holding on to your intuition, that corner stone of your foundation, can seem tenuous at best. But if you hold on, the storm will pass and you will become stronger for the experience. Don't be pulled into the force of the tide of emotions, distractions and shadows. These can cause you to doubt your very identity and the meaning of your existence. If you are pulled by the external gravitational force that demands your assimilation, you could incorporate cultural values and attitudes which may promise acceptance into a majority perspective, but will never guarantee your happiness and inclusion. You may be tossed around in the angry waters of uncertainty until you re-anchor yourself to what is permanent and true about your true identity.

Learn to see the trials and tribulations of life as a gift. It is in this fashion that you discover your intended purpose and potential. You can come to this process of self discovery by navigating the rough, turbulent waters of uncertainty or you can come to this point of self discovery through grateful celebration of your strength in the midst of new experiences. Fighting, suffering and struggling during this process of self transformation might be inevitable, but it is also optional.

You Are Already Rich

Regardless of your background, race, color, religion or economic buying power, all the knowledge that the world has ever accumulated is rightly yours simply because you are who you are. Knowledge is the most valuable and permanent of all currencies. Keep yourself thirsty for the waters of knowledge and the bread of truth. Gather information from as many sources as you can, however you can and expand your mind. Knowledge is found, not just in books, but in the experiences that life has to offer. Do not allow anyone or anything to keep you from accumulating knowledge and learn from the world around you. The more knowledge you accumulate the clearer you will be able to see the divine pattern operating in and through all things.

No person, no situation or power can keep you from your divine destiny. Unlock the code. Decipher the language of the collective creative power and there is nothing in the world you cannot obtain. The ONE source of all has gifted you with the bounty of life. Remember that the experience of separateness, poverty and isolation takes place in a mind that is fearful and limited by lack of awareness. These thoughts become embedded in the mind because the mind believes in the perception of a reality defined by the limited physical senses.

Reality is an endless sea of possibilities that cannot be fully understood with just these senses. Look around you. The universe communicates in abundance. There are billions of grains of sand on a beach, just as there are billions of stars and planets in the universe. You are like the sea and its countless drops of water. You are an indivisible part of something so great and so powerful that your mind simply cannot fully comprehend the greatness of your source. In your fear and limited thinking, you may frequently feel alone and isolated. Isolation is simply a thought of separation. How can a drop of water in the ocean feel itself different and apart from the powerful waves that carry it gently to the shore or hurl it violently against the rocks which melt upon the persistent force? The drop of water knows no distinction. It knows no separation. It is as much a part of the ocean as the entire body to which it belongs.

Unlike you, a drop of water has no free will or self awareness. Because you have free will, you are able to choose the life you dare to imagine, if you can but hold the image of your potential as a constant. This sense of self awareness or agency is the spark that allows you to co-create your reality with the ultimate Creator. Whether the choices you make leads to a positive or to a negative outcome is irrelevant. You are allowed to do with your life as you please. If you focus your thoughts on your failures and limitations, the seeds of disappointment will grow. Celebrate your success and recognize the passing moments of pleasure and joy. Be grateful when these moments occur and you will increase the likelihood of these occurring with greater frequency. Think of your mind as the ground and your thoughts as the seeds you plant. The ground never questions the planted seed. The ground simply receives all seeds with equal receptivity.

Life is a series of tumbles and falls. The wise person is not the one who makes no mistakes. The wise person may fall constantly, but learns something different, however small, with each subsequent fall. What you perceive as failure can be a great teacher if you listen with kind compassion to the lessons being taught. Without the truth of who you are, without the myths that accurately speak to your true, undistorted divine origin, you may begin to adopt the distorted myths of inferiority. You cannot pretend or aspire to be anything else other than that which you truly are. Yet, who you truly are is the ultimate mystery. In order to figure out who you truly are, you have to learn to tune out the noise and the constant external demands for your surrender, compliance and allegiance to a false identity. Learn to look inward and see yourself as the Creator sees you. Suspend your thinking and unify your mind with the force of creation. This force represents the ultimate mystery and your true source of power.

Lesson: Never Stop Dreaming

Greed and hunger for power have repeatedly displaced many of our ancestors and today we are still wandering, searching for a home and a place where we might live in peace. Our lands may no longer belong to us nor may the history and mythology left to us by our ancestors. Yet to spend the rest of our existence in anger, resentment and a desire for revenge is not the answer. The more anger you harbor, the more frustrated and miserable you will be. The only solution to our centuries of pain is the recognition that the wealth and freedom we seek is not found anywhere in the material world, but within ourselves.

Every culture in the world has created an expression and impression of God based on those aspects that most resemble the group's collective experience, their culture and surrounding reality. God is the collective mind of humanity and reigns within the throne of your individual mind. God is personal and must be personal to all. You must feel that the Creator is readily accessible, receptive and responsive. You do not need to fear the source and giver of your thoughts nor do you need a mediator to communicate with such awesome power. You are the embodiment of the one spirit, the one source of all life, the one creator. You are the "I AM". Since there is just ONE and since you are a child of the ONE, then all that you can imagine, all that you can hold in your dreams is possible if you hold in your mind the constant image of your desires. Hold firm to your vision and do not allow external events to sway you from your heart's desire. Insist and persist. Stay true to the vision of your heart's desire and your efforts will always be rewarded. Don't ever lose the ability to dream. Within the essence of your dreams is the power of creation.

Etched on the face of the Aztec Calendar is the history of your creation. According to ancient texts, across the span of time, the world has been destroyed and rebuilt four separate times. This is a mythical legend that speaks to the constant evolution of mankind. We are currently living in the fifth and final world, governed by the Fifth Sun. In this fifth world, the children of the sun will evolve and rise. The sons and daughters of the Fifth Sun will leap from a limited consciousness and a limited material world into the boundless reality of spiritual transformation.

The Creator is embodied as Tonatiuh, the Fifth Sun and as such, HE promises the light of awareness in your lifetime. You can reach the point of enlightenment and freedom here and now, without having to die or tolerate further punishment.

The promise of the Fifth Sun has been cast in stone and has been protected for centuries so that you could decode and apply the living word to your daily life. You are the incarnation of holy words spoken long ago. These are the words your great ancestors left carved on indestructible stones. These are the same ancestors that mapped the eternity of the universe and replicated it on earth, in the form of great buildings, temples and sacred pyramids that would perfectly mimic the movements of the planets and stars. Of all the greatest achievements of your ancestors, the message and promise of your liberation is the most valued treasure. The promise of your own liberation can be obtained by staying focused on the permanency of truth and ignoring the endless demands of Ollin, the agent of constant change.

Let go of all the cluttered thoughts and all the held resentments of past hurts because such thoughts do not serve you. In a crowded home, even a truck load of fine furniture is of little use. You must get rid of all the junk you have accumulated to make room for the new.

Every day there is greater evidence suggesting that the physical world is merely a field of manifestation of our inner thoughts.

All that you perceive in the material world begins at some point as a thought, an idea in your mind. Your mind is able to perceive "reality" based on memories of objects, experiences and stories previously reinforced by others. Your habitual thoughts of poverty and lack, the constant rumination about what is missing in your life, keep you from attracting goodness and abundance. There is a way out of this cycle of oppression and lack. Rather than waiting for society to fix the wrongs you see, rather than waiting around for social justice or the next great civil rights leader, stand as an example of one life lived according to its own principles. Rather than waiting around for your external environment to recognize your worth, be the agent of change in your own life.

More than ever, the world is clamoring, asking you to wake to the importance of living the present moment. More than ever before, it is important to recognize that the next giant leap of human evolution consists of the transformation of your own consciousness and the recognition of your intricate connection to all creation. Don't wait for those around you to catch up with the progressive and revolutionary thinking that declares "all humans are created equal." By changing the manner in which you think about yourself you will greatly impact the direction of your life. By becoming mindful of your thoughts and the manner in which they determine your reality, you will unlock the code to your potential. Identify damaging and limiting thoughts, replace these with thoughts more in line with the universal truth and ancestral principles and you will inevitably see a dramatic improvement in the quality of your life. By reclaiming the myths and legends of your ancestors, you will know that the ancestors lived in constant communion with all of creation and were not the barbarians and violent savages recorded in an inaccurate history. There is a treasure of knowledge in the teachings of the elders that is meant to heal your soul.

Go back to your beginning and familiarize yourself with the source that created you. Know that this energy, this power operates for good and that it always multiplies, always says "yes" to your most sincere requests. You can achieve the unimaginable. While this achievement might require persistence and hard work, know that you are resilient. Knowing you are capable of impacting your own change is as easy as looking in the mirror and knowing who truly is looking back at you. The spirit of the Creator, the Great Ancestor, wants you to have all that you desire, all that you dare dream of having, all that is rightly yours. Watch your requests and keep in mind that you must be clear and consistent with what you are asking. Stop asking for things and their opposite at the same time. Stop blocking your own abundance and joy. Stop being afraid of asking for something and then believing you are not deserving. If and when you ask for something, make room in your life to welcome and receive it. Know that all you dare imagine is possible because you are the sons and daughters of the ONE Creator and you share the ONE consciousness and mind.

This is the message of your divine heritage. Be willing to let go of fear. Be willing to forget all your limitations and short comings. Be willing to remember your true identity. Be willing to honor your ancestors by reclaiming their promise to you. Reclaim the true treasures of *Moctezuma*. Reclaim the treasures of lost cities of gold. Reclaim the power to recreate and renew your life. Liberate yourself as you liberate your limited understanding and conception of the divine.

As your mind becomes still, you will regain and reclaim your right to breathe, your right to fill your lungs with the truth. Hold on to your center and learn to calm the run away beast that hides within your rampant thoughts. Don't hold on to your pain thinking that it somehow makes you different or unique.

We've all been hurt, some of us worse than others. Don't let thoughts of pain take over your life. You must not let your mind throw you and knock you down.

We live in an ever shrinking world. The price of housing and the demands for food and natural resources dwindle with each passing day. Borders and walls are erected and humans are categorized according to their economic viability in a world market. This division dehumanizes us all. It divides the world into those that feel oppressed and denied and those that live in fear of being invaded, ever afraid that an entitled way of life is slipping away.

We've all been taught to sacrifice. Ancestral women have often sacrificed it all, giving of their bodies and themselves to secure the well-being of the next generation. They have told themselves that "as long as my children have, and my family is alright, that is all that really matters to me." Many men sacrifice as well. Our sacrifice is our voice and our sensibilities. We hide our feelings and our emotions behind a mask of bravado and strength, a badge of masculinity that does not allow room for tears or any expression of emotion or vulnerability which might be viewed as weakness. Men desire a connection to others but often feel inadequate and weak if they have to verbalize their thoughts. Along the way, you can lose the language of emotions and become numb to life. Denied of a native language and mode of expression, the ancestral past still longs to communicate the basic truth of our deep connection to life. Your inner voice has been clouded by the noise and the distractions of daily life. To reconnect with the source of your power and happiness, you must be able to reconnect with that central voice of your intuition.

Lesson: Uncover your Voice-Tell Your Story

To uncover your inner voice is to understand your own personal story and the themes that emerge from that discovery. Ask yourself how your personal myth perpetuates your suffering. Are you aware of your own story? As you sit with a friend, what do you reveal about yourself, your view of life and social relationships? Listen as a detached observer to your own tale. Hear yourself recount the story from your childhood to your present. Remember that everyone has suffered and that there is no prize for the winner. Can you begin to identify the common themes that repeat themselves throughout? Can you see how these themes continue to repeat themselves through your relationships and life circumstances? Make a conscious decision that your personal story of suffering and lack must change.

Work hard everyday to realize your dreams but detach yourself from any expectation. Often you can become so caught up in how something is supposed to look that you miss the possibility for something even greater emerging. You no longer need to struggle and strive. You are the embodiment and the promise entrusted to one generation after another by grandfathers Quetzalquatl and Huichilopotchli. You are the end of darkness and confusion. You are the resurrection and the word made flesh. You are to rise from the depths of the darkness that stirs in your mind and you are to be lifted upward into the heavenly realm where light, clarity and truth prevail.

Lesson: Listen

Can you hear the whisperings? Can you hear your name being called, asking you to awaken to your true identity? Do you have the courage to say yes and step forward and proudly, without fear and with willingness, embrace your true potential? Can you claim and accept your divine inheritance? Can you put your outstretched arms in front of you so that you might be able to receive the overflow that is freely and joyfully given to you? Hold as much as you can grasp and when you are unable to hold any more, know that there is still so much more for you to receive.

Why do you still toil and suffer, enslaved in poverty and misery, when you are a child of the Divine. You have no one to convince of your true worth and true identity but yourself. Stop trying to find acknowledgement and recognition from those around you who are shrouded by their own confusion and darkness. The moment that you recognize that you are the alchemical energy and the source, capable of transforming dust into gold, you will come to know your true identity. The moment you realize that you hold the key that opens your self-imposed prison right in the palm of your hand, you will be set free.

People have fought to the death for their freedom, their pride and their honor, but there is no need to use violence to obtain the liberating results you seek. Today, you need to learn to use information and education to effect change in your life. Use the knowledge of the universal laws which work consistently and impersonally. You must recognize that you are part of a greater whole. Unite your voice and knowledge with that of your brothers and sisters and you will be able to achieve the unimaginable. You must learn to optimize the power of your word and the power of your inner force. When used appropriately, this inner force will exercise greater power than any weapon you can wield.

Lesson: Claim Your Heritage

There is great strength in claiming the legacy of your past. There is a deep sense of completeness and a power of home surges through your veins. The claiming of that heritage begins with the reclaiming of your self as a worthy recipient. Modern children of the Fifth Sun are a mixture of the old and new worlds and cultures. You are the power of the past and the infinite potential of an eternal future. Your existence and your perception of reality are determined by how you understand the presence of two bloods in your veins and two perceptions of the world that lives through your mind. Being able to hold multiple views of reality, viewing life through multiple cultural frames, can free you from the rigid beliefs that the world and reality can only be perceived and understood through one dominant perspective. Your voice is necessary and valid because you hold an alternative perspective essential to properly understand the web of creation. Recognize that you represent the unity of races. You are a direct reflection of the universal force of creation and the oppressive and punitive images of God constructed by a limiting past. That myth of limitation can now be cast away. Your personal journey of self discovery is also a rediscovery of the oneness at the core of our extended human family.

For more than twenty-five thousand years, the souls of your relations have traversed these lands. Their journey on earth left their mark etched permanently upon the large and small trails carved out of these most sacred hills and meadows. The land calls to you because it claims you as a legitimate heir and a child of the Fifth Sun. Your loving great grandmothers, grandfathers, mothers, and fathers have exhausted their bodies in fields and work camps, surrendering their souls in silent whisperings carried by the wind. Their lives stand as a testimony of the value inherent in preserving these treasures of the past. All the efforts of your elders have accumulated to assure that the message was delivered to you across the span of time, space and matter.

As the children of this fifth world, governed by this Fifth Sun, we are poised to take the next quantum leap in the evolution of the human race. This quantum leap of evolution will take place when we recognize and realize our true imbedded potential. Our transformation will take place when we learn to read the significance of the encoded history left behind by all those ancestors who have contributed to our embodiment. Let us take this quantum leap in human evolution and begin to uncover the rich treasure that has been entrusted to us within our consciousness and awareness.

In This Moment: I Offer You My Dream

Last night I dreamed that my grandmother Lidia came to visit me. She sat on a chair in my living room. She asked how I was. I held a book of stories in my right hand. I told her I had been reading a story about a young boy who fell in love with a bull. I was telling her the story, but I knew that I was really speaking about myself. I told her how this boy loved this bull so much; that the bull became his best friend, his brother, his protector, even his god. Eventually the boy grew up and the bull became old and died. The boy, now a young man, was devastated by his loss.

My grandmother pressed her lips and nodding her head curiously, asked me, "What do you think that story means?"

I said, "I guess it means you can learn to love and adore anything, even an old bull."

She gripped her chin and said, "Hum... I guess you can look at it that way. Or you can believe that God pretended to be a bull and spoke to the boy in that disguise. You see, Son, God can only reveal itself to you in a manner that you can understand. You are a child in love with a bull and so God expresses through your love of that great powerful force. The real God would not fit in your mind." Grandma Lidia smiled at me. She rocked back and forth in her chair and fell back asleep.

I watched her sleep peacefully as I flipped the pages of the story book. The book was full of illustrations of constellations of stars. The stars formed written messages that interpreted their celestial meaning. One of these constellations drew my attention. I looked at it and as I did, the stars suddenly moved to create a message that read, "You have been experiencing trouble finding yourself. You have been struggling with a force with which you should not struggle. Learn to befriend this force and look around you. There is no more need to try and be. You are already there!"

I have come to believe that life is lived in two parts. The first part of life is a series of experiences in which we might frequently encounter great pain and great disappointments. The second part of life is learning about the gift contained within the pain and the treasures embedded in the lessons and disappointments of the past. Every painful experience has a purpose and the purpose of life on this earth is to determine the lessons that lead us to freedom. These lessons are often trapped in the experienced pain and suffering. As you step back and appreciate the pattern and sequence of unfolding events, you will be able to witness a rhythm and natural intelligence to all life. The ancestors' dream is realized in you. You are the promise fulfilled. Open your eyes. Wake up and live the dream.

ABOUT THE AUTHOR

Dr. Jorge Partida

Clinical and Research Psychologist

Dr. Jorge Partida was born in Guadalajara, Jalisco, Mexico and immigrated to the Chicago area when he was nine years old. Throughout his childhood, Dr. Jorge was greatly influenced by the teachings of his grandmother who taught him the healing arts of the past.

Dr. Jorge is a national and international consultant, providing services to education, government, employment and religious communities interested in working with those most in need. For more than ten years, Dr. Jorge has been a regular television and radio presenter and public speaker. Additionally, Dr. Jorge has served as Vice President of Research and Development for Human Resources Development Institute, Inc. (HRDI), a large behavioral health care organization in Chicago. He has been a regular consultant for Migrant Education, an organization dedicated to helping sons of migrant workers succeed in education. Much of Dr. Jorge's clinical work has focused on assisting young Latinos navigate challenges related to gang violence, incarceration, family reunification, and access to health and education.

Dr. Jorge worked for the San Francisco Department of Public

Health (SFDPH) as the Director of Substance Abuse Services and Deputy Director of Behavioral Health and also served as Director of the Doctorate Program in Clinical Psychology at John F. Kennedy University, California. In addition to his clinical work, Dr. Jorge is the founding President of "Los Compadres Sin Fronteras", a non-profit group that focuses on increasing economic development and social empowerment of Latino men and their families.

For more information on Dr. Jorge and his work, please visit **www.drjorge.net**

LaVergne, TN USA
16 October 2009
161107LV00003B/2/P